DRESSING SHIP

Also by Janet Groene

Cooking on the Go
How to Live Aboard a Boat

DRESSING SHIP

How to Furnish, Refurbish, and Accessorize Your Boat

Janet Groene

Hearst Marine Books
New York

NAPERVILLE PUBLIC LIBRARIES
Naperville, IL

Recognizing the importance of preserving what has been written, it is the policy of William Morrow and Company, Inc., and its imprints and affiliates to have the books it publishes printed on acid-free paper, and we exert out best efforts to that end.

Library of Congress Cataloging-in-Publication Data

Groene, Janet.
    Dressing ship : how to furnish, refurbish, and accessorize your
  boat / Janet Groene.
        p.   cm.
    Includes index.
    ISBN 0-688-09517-8
    1. Yachts and yachting—Furniture, equipment, etc.
    I. Title.
  VM331.G76   1991
  623.8'2223—dc20   90-5032
                                                       CIP

Printed in the United States of America

First Edition

1   2   3   4   5   6   7   8   9   10

BOOK DESIGN BY ARLENE GOLDBERG

Contents

Introduction

Yacht decorators and designers talk a slick, chic lingo that dances with ideals, dotes on romance, delights in theory. That's all well and good ashore, but you and I are boat owners. While we'd like to be rhapsodizing about mauve and aubergine, our language leans more toward words like dry rot, mildew, algae, knockdowns, diesel soot, corrosion, leaks, rust, beating to windward, and getting pooped.

Pretty is as pretty does.

This book is a guide to products and techniques that will make life aboard your yacht more comfortable, more swank, and more in pace with today's opulent life-style, but without compromising the kinds of materials, preservatives, placement, and construction that are demanded by the serious, seagoing, pleasure boat.

Dressing Ship is not a guide to cute new shades of chintz. Nor is it a how-to for the ship's carpenter, electrician, or painter. It is for all men and women who want a more liveable boat, both those who are working with a professional decorator and those who are doing some or all of the work themselves.

Our theoretical boat is in the thirty-five-foot to sixty-five-foot range. Her owners like to get the most for their money and want to spend it with a view not only to today's comforts but to tomorrow's maintenance, good looks, and resale.

While styles and tastes tend to change slowly, technology is in constant revolution. So, it's here that the yacht owner most needs guidance in taking advantage of exciting new marine materials and techniques.

No matter how extravagantly you intend to decorate your boat, or how tightly you must pinch pennies, this book will lead you through questions, answers, solutions, and decisions. My hope is that the resulting boat will bring you years of pleasure, fewer of the wrong kinds of surprises, and enduring value.

Apologia

It may seem to some readers that this book includes a large number of household items at the expense of time-proven marine equipment. My long-term readers know that I have always favored the use of the best, marine-quality materials and equipment. A good marine air conditioner, heating system, generator, or galley stove has no competitor from comparable household appliances.

It must be realized, however, that many modern products *can* come aboard without compromising quality, safety, strength, and durability. And likewise, some items that are designed for marine use end up ashore. Many products, though advertised and marketed only to homeowners, are as at home on a boat as they are in a mountain lodge or a beach cottage. Others would perish in the marine environment.

My aim is to give you as wide a choice as possible, assuming that you'll make the best choice for your own boat. Furnishing a thirty-five-foot sailboat for a circumnavigation will be quite a different project from decorating a houseboat that will never leave Tennessee.

Some readers will be offended by my use of such landlubber terms as floor, wall, bathroom, ceiling, door, closet, and window.

I am familiar with nautical terms; my closest friends might even admit that my sailing vocabulary extends to a saltiness somewhat beyond that of a lady's needs. Where appropriate, I've used nautical references.

However, in the interests of clarity when discussing furnishings and decor, I've used whatever terms are most likely to be used by your decorator and by the suppliers of furnishings and materials.

To paraphrase Winston Churchill, to say "head" when I mean toilet and "head" when I mean bathroom, is a form of errant pedantry up with which I will not put.

—Janet Groene

Decor: What's Ahead

In summing up decorating trends for the 1990's, *Home* magazine began with a surprise. "A dumpster in the driveway" is the new status symbol, the magazine said. This and other life-style trends are as true for boats as they are for homes. The need for recycling and trash management is sure to play an increasing role in galley design, just as entertainment electronics are shaping our saloons, and the popularity of spas and fitness machines requires that our bathrooms—areas which can hardly any longer be called heads—be larger and more luxurious.

Only a generation ago, we would have smirked at any suggestion that a pleasure boat should be anything but a floating summer camp—austere, practical, furnished with castoffs, and bare of any sissy touches. We progressed into an age of creature comforts afloat, but even these were trimmed in brass and brightwork, were nautically themed ad nauseam, and had color schemes that centered around red, white, and blue.

Next came an era of miniaturization, in which entire living rooms, dining rooms, bars, libraries, dens, pantries, and harem-size bedrooms were shrunk and stuffed into a hull. They had eye appeal in the showroom, but were as livable as a doll house—and not much more durable.

3

Say hello to a new age in yacht decor.

Today we expect more plush boat interiors, sized for real people, in tones that are more tasteful, less strident, and more homelike. And we can have them without sacrificing seagoing durability, thanks to brawny new plastics, effective waterproofers, tough wood finishes, stainproof carpeting, fadeproof dyes, unbreakable mirrors, and much more.

Efficient new refrigeration and air conditioning, once bulky to install and expensive and clanky to operate, are now de rigueur on boats as small as twenty-one-footers. The most sophisticated consumer electronics, from CD players to VCRs, now come in 12V models and few families would go to sea without them. Rarely do you see a boat larger than twenty-one feet that does not have a microwave oven. Cellular phones are moving into the "necessity" category, too.

We all like to think that we go boating to get away from it all. But a quick tour of any boat show makes it clear that we yachties are more likely to take "it all" with us. Even the circumnavigators I've known are all ardent ham-radio operators, consumed with pressing "skeds" and constantly in touch with networks of like-minded souls.

As a former live-aboard, I know that life on a boat can be harsh, wet, sticky hot or clammy cold. Even in the best of times, there are the assaults of mildew, salt spray, and merciless sun. At its worst, the sea is a rampaging demon that can throw your floating home on her beam ends, crack holes in her hull, and send winds and spume shrieking through the most carefully contrived decor.

Now, however, thanks to new products and new protectants for traditional products, the yachtsman is able to live with the beauty of both worlds—surrounded by the sea in all its harsh realities, yet cupped in the comforts of a gracious, but enduring and practical, home.

Looking Ahead

It's a good idea to think in terms of current and future life-style trends, so you can create a floating environment that will be practical for years to come.

Here is just one example of what I mean. Trash management has turned from a routine boating chore into a serious matter of compliance, in many areas, with strict laws governing how discards must be separated, disposed of, and recycled.

Many boat designers allow no room at all for a trash bin. You have to find room in a corner or under the sink for a wastebasket. Other decorators design in one of the new, downsize compactors under galley counters. Yet, depending on where you do most of your boating, you may need not one waste center but several—one for glass, one for paper, one for plastics, another for aluminum, and so on. Otherwise, you'll have the unpleasant job of separating everything after off-loading it. To fail to do so could violate local or state laws.

In all the boats I've been aboard, I've seen only a handful that provided for such sorting, and they assumed only two categories: Man-made products were separated from garbage, which was thrown overboard. Today it's illegal to throw anything over the side. If you have a garbage disposal, it will lead to rapid filling of your holding water tank. And, if food scraps must be stowed, you soon have an odor problem.

Think twice about adding a garbage disposal or a compactor. Either could complicate, rather than comply, depending on where you dock and how you empty your holding tank(s). The more thought and space you can devote to trash containment, the better, because the green revolution is just beginning.

The Palette

Today's look down below is lighter, with less mahogany and teak and more fabric. Dee Robinson, of Dee Robinson Custom Yacht

Interiors in Fort Lauderdale, told *Marine Business Journal* that wood and metal are popular accents, with lighter woods such as bleached oak becoming popular. "I feel a light palette works for spaciousness, but I use a lot of dark accents," she said.

You have only to remember color crazes of the past to realize how quickly decor can be stalled in one decade or another by fad colors. You can't find towels today to coordinate with some of the popular bath-fixture colors of ten years ago, or kitchen accessories to go with appliance colors that have come and gone.

In my own projects, I stick with white or very neutral, light colors for items which will be very difficult to change, such as the galley sink and stove, countertops, tiles, wall coverings, head fixtures, and the wood portions of built-in furniture. An entire new look can be achieved by changing only the upholstery, carpeting, window coverings, the towels and shower curtain, or other accessories which are easily replaced.

Fabrics and Materials

Designers are going daffy for the new laminates or micas, and for good reason. They are durable, scrubbable, virtually mildew-proof, flexible, and are available in hundreds of colors, designs, patterns, qualities, reflectances, textures, and in imitation and real woods. Give the chapter that discusses laminates a thoughtful read, then visit a number of decorators and home stores to get a thorough knowledge of the amazing laminates marketplace.

Easy-care fabrics are a fact of life, but the natural look will probably remain "in" for years to come. As a result, manufacturers are offering fine choices in cottons, linens, silks, and wools which are combined with synthetics for longer wear and easier cleaning.

At the same time, synthetics are looking better than ever and clean more easily. Some, such as the olefins which are used for marine carpeting and wall covering, are almost impossible to stain or destroy.

The choice in marine vinyls is high, wide, and handsome, and they are stronger and easier to clean than ever before. The shiny ones, now pearlized, are shinier; the matte finishes are more muted; the textures are more nearly like the leather or alligator they pretend to be.

At the same time, the demand for real leathers among manufacturers of furniture and cars means a bigger choice of better and more practical leathers, skins, and furs for marine decorators, and they are using them lavishly.

Tile, the toughest and most timeless of coverings for walls, countertops, and galley and shower walls, has never been as popular in North America as it has always been in Europe, but it is catching up here. The result is an enormously expanded choice of sizes, styles, and colors for many uses aboard a yacht.

New countertops include Corian, 2000X, and Avonite. They look like marble and wear like iron. New carpetings are thick, luxurious, and nearly indestructible. Other floorings you can choose from include practical new woods, vinyls, and rubber. In only a few years, we've moved out of the teak, plastic, and canvas age into an era of a wide variety of rugged, high-tech, materials.

The Bath

During the 1970s and 1980s, extra bathrooms were a passionate priority with architects on land and sea. Boats that a few years ago may have had a portable potty and a curtain now had enclosed heads. Boats that would have had one head were now appearing with two or more. Then, toward the end of the eighties bathrooms began to grow from add-ons into real rooms.

Within ten years, the average new household bathroom grew by one hundred square feet. It was during this time that I began to notice the appearance on boats of spas and whirlpools. With increasing interest in fitness, home bathrooms grew larger and more luxurious, especially in regard to saunas, soaking tubs, spas, and a workout machine or two. This trend carried over almost immediately into boats, where spas are commonly seen both on deck and in master staterooms.

Ready-made reinforced plastic showers and tub "surrounds" are available in so many sizes and shapes for homes, you may be able to add one at far less than the cost of a custom fiberglass shower. Dozens of shower sprays are available, most of them with a water-saving feature once found only on boats but now common in homes. Wall-mounted hair dryers, made for use in homes and hotels, are ideal for the space-pinched boat owner.

After years of confusion over what would happen with holding-tank laws and applications, the industry has settled down and is offering a wide choice of marine toilets in all sizes, shapes, colors, and types ranging from recirculating to vacuum-flush models. And, if you can't find what you need in the marine market, there is a mammoth choice in the RV realm.

The Galley

Small kitchens are out and the big, family kitchen is back. Both husbands and wives cook. Everyone gathers 'round, and meal preparation often becomes a team affair. So it's more appropriate today to opt for a galley that is incorporated into the saloon, rather than a separate galley where the cook is isolated from the flow of conversation. On many boats, this is easily done simply by providing a bar or counter where once a wall or pass-through would have been put up, and by otherwise leaving more open space.

The first downdraft stove (high volumes of air are drawn down over the cooking surface, removing heat and odors through a vent) I ever saw was in a sailboat galley. Now Jenn-Air has introduced an electric downdraft cooktop which has been approved for outdoor use on patios and decks, underscoring increasing interest in downdraft cooking and providing an alternative to the barbecue for protected deck spaces. Modern Maid offers a full size, gas, downdraft range.

In reading the section on stoves, you'll explore the possibilities of multiple energy sources—a gas cooktop, microwave oven, and self-cleaning electric oven, for example. Propane stoves are readily accepted now by most boat owners; the increasing use of generators makes electric cooking more popular; the loathsome alcohol stove has improved; time-honored kerosene and diesel stoves are still a very practical, salty choice for the serious voyager.

Stainless-steel sinks come in more qualities, shapes, and sizes than ever before. Porcelain sinks, in a choice of colors, are back. Widespread use of clear acrylics lightens the galley and makes it seem more spacious. Through household appliance manufacturers, you now have a wide choice of conveniences such as dishwashers, compactors, freezers, and icemakers in downsize models. And, through recreational vehicle suppliers, more appliances than ever are now available in 12V or propane models.

More Trends

Probably the largest single revolution in modern yacht living is electronics, which *Southern Living* magazine called "today's hearth." In planning a saloon, placement of the radio, tape decks, turntables, speakers, television, and VCR should be plotted as carefully as chairs and settees. Lighting is part of the equation. Artificial lighting should enhance TV viewing, listening to music, or conversation. Yet the TV should be placed where outdoor light won't glare on it—not an easy assignment in a sunlit saloon.

In reading individual chapters, you'll learn about how trends ashore such as apartment living, mobile homes, RVs, and the growing influence of European and Japanese style, have made it easier to add to your yacht some item that was never before available. For example, zero-clearance and ventless fireplaces sold for use in small homes and apartments make it possible to have a fireplace now in a houseboat or powerboat saloon.

There has never been a more exciting time to own a boat, and to turn that boat into a real home—for the weekend, for the season, for a voyage, or for a circumnavigation.

Chapter 1

WORKING WITH (AND WITHOUT) A DECORATOR

"Don't do it, period," replied Vicky Moses when I asked her how to work with an interior decorator who doesn't usually work with boats. "Find a decorator who knows boats and boating. Even if you live in an area where there are few boats, you can find a marine decorating specialist who will travel to where your boat is."

Moses, owner of Oceanic Designs in Daytona Beach, is both a boater and a decorator. Better still, she's a *re*decorator who knows not only what works in the ivory tower world of new boats, but what *doesn't* work because she has hauled away, stripped off, and chipped out enough rot, rusty staples, mildewed materials, and sagging draperies to sink a battleship.

Working with her partner, Kathy Sanders, Moses has designed interiors for a line of new Atlantic Yachts and has refurbished many boats, from a forty-two-foot Chris Craft Commander and a forty-two-foot Gulfstar to an elegant old Trumpy.

Vicky has been a boat owner since childhood, and has cruised the Bahamas as well as inland seas. She studied merchandising and was in retail clothing until she decided to go back to school to study interior design. There she met Kathy, and a business was born.

The two women do much of their own stripping, fabricating, and sewing, and in the beginning built their own furniture to fit tight spaces on the boats they were refurbishing. They continue to do their own measuring, drapery, some furniture building, and hands-on installation right down to the last stainless-steel staple and acrylic tieback.

Advises Vicky: "When you're shopping for a marine decorator to do or redo your boat, ask if the designer actually works aboard the boat, and is there to supervise installation. You know, many decorators do it all on the drawing board, then depend on their subcontractors to try to make things fit.

"We find that household drapery people simply can't measure boats. We do it ourselves to make sure the fit is exactly right. We're on the boat early in the game, working with electricians and carpenters to plan lighting and other decorator features that have to be done in concert with plumbing, wiring, and other basics.

"Everyone is so crazy for miniblinds," Vicky admits, "and we'll put them in if a client insists. But we won't warranty the hardware because there isn't a blind made that is all stainless through and through. We prefer to use tailored fabric draperies, with marine-quality drapery tracks top and bottom."

Vicky Moses voiced my views exactly. I've interviewed many decorators, including some who design for major boat manufacturers. Many know the design business thoroughly, but they may never have been out on a boat, don't know boating, don't understand the demands of the marine environment.

They design stylish interiors that have all the bells, whistles, and frills—and are about as seaworthy as a brick bungalow.

Here are some actual quotes from marine decorators:

"A room has to have an architectural coherence before you enter into color."

"It's very kinetic."

"We don't want to make a strong color statement this year... color takes a supportive role to design."

"The color, texture, and overall warmth...will not be perceived as a regional statement."

"Grays are becoming browner...pastels are becoming brighter and more saturated."

"People relate to woods..."

If you're like me, you read such statements as so much smokescreen gibberish. Instead, I ask how many rubs the carpeting is rated for on the Wyzenbeek scale, and whether a mildewcide was added to the adhesive when the bulkhead covering was installed.

The other problem with a designer who works only with pen and paper, is that he or she may not supervise surface preparations which are an essential step in redecorating with new headliners, laminates, paints, and some floor coverings.

In the chapters that follow, you'll see that every product that goes into a marine decorating or redecorating project has to be, first and foremost, chosen for the harsh demands of the boating environment. After reading this book and contacting several of the designers listed at the end of this chapter, you should have a sense of which designer is right for you, your life-style, your budget, and your boat.

What will decorating or redecorating cost? Less than you think. Moses' biggest project to date cost only twenty-eight thousand dollars. She can do wonders for six thousand to eight thousand dollars.

"You'd be surprised how many people come in here and expect a full proposal on speculation," Moses told me. "Measuring alone takes hours. Your decorator should provide preliminary sketches and a sample board, but a design fee should be paid for this. Some boat owners expect a designer to do a complete redo on paper so they can take it around to get the best bid. Designers have to be paid for their time and labor. In our case, we'll apply the design fee to the order if we get a contract from the client."

Learning the Lexicon

When I began interviewing marine decorators, there was an immediate communications gap. Most of my writings deal with categories and generic terms. Decorators, by contrast, are intensely brand loyal, their language sprinkled with trademarked names—some very local or little known—that they use generically to refer to a carpet pad or an upholstery suede.

If you think that all laminates are Formica, all interlinings are Pellon, and all whirlpools are Jacuzzis, you're immediately lost when a designer mentions Wilsonart or Swirl-way. Don't be daunted by jargon. Even the designers themselves may not know the difference between a filament polyester thread and an air-entangled polyester thread, or whether Ultimax is better than Star Ultra Dee.

Writers identify proprietary names with little R's and TM's and C's in circles. Marine decorators, by contrast, may lard their lingo with brand names which you've never heard of. There are many, many brands of most items, and many of them are chemically or mechanically similar.

Decorators will be brand loyal for many reasons, some of them important to your project and others that have nothing to do with you. Designers are as interested as you are in quality and wide choice, but they are also concerned with cost, markup, financial float, delivery time, supplier reliability, warranty fulfillment as it affects them as retailers, whether the distributor has a toll-free telephone number, and profit, profit, profit.

The more you, as the boat owner, can learn about materials, techniques, and generic names for brand products, the better partners you and your decorator can be.

Who Does the Work?

Some of you reading this book will do all your own decorating and redecorating. Others will do part of the work. Still others cannot, or should not, do anything more than write checks.

Every phase of a decorating project requires special expertise. We've all seen boats that had been finished by inept do-it-yourselfers. When Gordon and I were shopping for the boat that was to be our home, we looked at scores of boats that had been slapped with a fast face-lift in hopes of making a quick sale. Many had been badly botched, presenting the new buyer with hours of work in tearing out slapdash work before serious restoration could begin.

Since coordination is essential in every phase of the project, someone must orchestrate what may be a very complex series of events. Plumbing, wiring, and carpentry must be completed or stubbed in before the cornices are added or the countertops put on or the stove dropped in.

As your own contractor, you'll spend a lot more time at the boat and on the phone, and will probably sweat a few bullets on days when work gets out of sync. By using a professional marine decorator, you save hours of agony.

On the other hand, it's satisfying and money-saving to work on your own boat. In some instances, you can make trial runs with a color or accessory and take it back to the store if you don't like the way it fits in. You can shop sales, wangle best deals. And, for those boat owners who are truly expert in bosun skills, there is the added satisfaction of knowing that a job was done precisely right, with the right materials, from start to finish.

Should you work with a yacht decorator? It may be wiser, and cheaper, than you think.

Interior designers who specialize in boats include:

Anita's Interiors, 101 Shipyard Way, Newport Beach, CA 92663. Showrooms in Newport Beach and Long Beach.

Tom Bakker, 11136 Kendale Way, Delta, B.C., Canada V4C 3P5

Paulette Bean, 2051 N.W. 11th St., Miami, FL 33125

Anne Brengle, Design & Conservation, 24 N. Water St., New Bedford, MA 02740

Elizabeth Dalton, 2480 PGA Blvd., Suite 5, Palm Beach Gardens, FL 33410

Design Direction, 4648 Paul St., Philadelphia, PA 19124

Designer Marine, 1245 W. Pomono Rd., Corona, CA 91720

Suzanne DeVall, 1234 S.E. Union Ave., Portland, OR 97214

Devlin Design Group, 2398 San Diego Ave., San Diego, CA 92110

Diana Yacht Design Inc., 324 Datura St., Suite 230, West Palm Beach, FL 33401

Dieter Empacher, 75 Evans Rd., Marblehead, MA 01945

Laurie Diner, 407 S. Pineapple Ave., Sarasota, FL 34236

First Impressions Industries Inc., 12564 N.W. 14th Ave., North Miami, FL 33161

Four Seas Boatique Ltd., 154 E. Boston Post Rd., Mamaroneck, NY 10543

Fryco Inc., 7107 Silver Leaf Lane, Houston, TX 77088

Glade Johnson Design Inc., 11820 Northup Way, Suite 220, Bellevue, WA 98005

Granata Design, 10 Cookers Hawk, Hilton Head, SC 29928

Steven Gurowitz, 1612 N.W. 23rd Ave., Fort Lauderdale, FL 33310

Harbor Master Yacht Interiors, 221 Dufferin St., Suite 105N, Toronto, Ont., Canada M6K 1Y9

J.B. Hargrave Naval Architects Inc., 205½ 6th St., West Palm Beach, FL 33401

Ron Hill, 855 San Remo Rd., Pasadena, CA 91105

Inside Designs Ltd., 3200 S. Square Shopping Center, New Bern, NC 28560

International Marine Designs Inc., 7341 Garden Grove Blvd., Garden Grove, CA 92641

Diane LaSauce, 2814 S. Wakefield St., Arlington, VA 22206

Arron Latt Associates, 9808 Wilshire Blvd, Beverly Hills, CA 90212

Oceanic Designs, 224 S. Beach St., Suite 203, Daytona Beach, FL 32114

Pedrick Yacht Designs Inc., 3 Ann St., Newport, RI 02840

Plachter Interior Design Studio, 1600 S.E. 17th St., Suite 310, Fort Lauderdale, FL 33316

POSH Inc., 19 Bliss Mine Rd., Middletown, RI 02840

Susan Puelo, 2101 S. Andrews Ave., #104, Fort Lauderdale, FL 33316

Hallie Rogers Rugg, Below Decks Inc., 250 15th Ave. S., St. Petersburg, FL 33701

Shipmate Interiors, 20873 Paloma, St. Clair Shores, MI 48080

Augusto Villalon, 1927 S.W. Pine Island Rd., Cape Coral, FL 33991.

Rob Webb, Design Centre, 100 Leader Heights Rd., York, PA 17403.

Yacht Interiors of Annapolis Inc., 326 First St., Suite 12, Annapolis, MD 21403

Yacht Interiors of Essex, 7 S. Cove Lane, Essex, CT 06426

Chapter 2

~~~~~~

GOING FOR THE PERFECT GALLEY

~~~~~~

Some things never change. The sea, seagoing people, tastes in foods, and space limitations are the same today as they were a generation ago. In other areas changes have been so dramatic, we hardly know where to begin in bringing the galley into the twenty-first century.

Computer catalogs offer programs that give complete nutritional analysis or provisioning help. New stoves can microwave or steam foods in mere seconds. New ready-to-eat meals were irradiated to last for months without refrigeration. New plastic bakeware can be used at temperatures up to 450 degrees.

New marine refrigeration is superefficient to cool down faster using less energy; new eutectic plates hold longer when the power is off. New household refrigerators, which are often chosen for the 110V galley, are superlight and ultracompact and they include such conveniences as beverage dispensers and automatic ice makers.

Probably the biggest problem for the seagoing homemaker is, and always will be, finding enough space. Luckily, the marketplace offers a great many dual-purpose items: the ceramic cooktop

Coated steel racks allow for drainage and air circulation in lockers, iceboxes, and refrigerators. Placed in sinks, such racks protect the sink from being scratched when items are stowed in them underway.
RUBBERMAID

which serves as counter space when cold; the combination convection-microwave oven; appliances that hang up under cupboards; European laundry appliances that wash, then dry, in the same machine; and multipurpose appliances that use one motor to run long lists of accessories from mixer and juicer to grinder and food processor.

One of the most important changes in recent years has been the way waste products are dealt with. Only a few years ago, everything went overboard. Today, national and international laws prohibit ocean dumping and, when you get to shore with the trash and garbage, it must be separated into three or more categories.

One of my pet peeves in galley design is that there is often no room for a wastebasket. Now, even more space is needed for separate bags to collect plastic, paper, glass, aluminum, and garbage discards. If you're designing or redesigning a galley from scratch, don't neglect this increasingly important feature. Though the situation is bound to change, right now we're seeing an increase in convenience foods in bulky packages and disposable pouches or pans—increasing our trash load just at a time when marinas are starting to get tougher about trash collection.

Plastic storage bins are available in many sizes and shapes, to provide waterproof storage for everything from linens to trash, clothing to tools. RUBBERMAID

Drawer liners keep galleyware organized and quiet underway. This two-tier cutlery tray gives a bonus storage area. RUBBERMAID

One of my longtime complaints is that galley ventilation in production boats is often inadequate. A naval architect who has never cooked a meal on a boat doesn't understand how quickly heat builds up on a hot day, in a small galley, under a low overhead. Now, during the earliest stages of a refit, is the best time to add whatever ventilators, dorade boxes, solar fans, or other air exchangers you can manage.

For comfort's sake, you're concerned with getting hot air out of the galley. To prevent the build-up of mildew and grease, you also want cooking steam and spatters to exit the galley by the shortest route.

A spatter shield over the stove isn't enough. Nor is a recirculating exhaust fan 100 percent effective, no matter what filters it contains. If possible, design in a good, high-volume (expressed in cfm, or cubic feet per minute) overboard exhaust fan. If a fan isn't feasible, try to add a low-profile ventilator (available through marine catalogs) or an old-fashioned Charley Noble (a leakproof chimney). Your galley may be midget-size, but you'll be making full-size meals with all the steam, stains, billowing heat, and spatters that such meals create.

Galley ventilation, like lighting, which is described in another chapter, must be incorporated in your earliest planning so that wiring, ducting, and carpentry can be allowed for.

Galley Layout

Cooking centers are usually designed so that the sink, refrigerator, and stove create a triangle. The object is to use the least motion whether you're going from refrigerator to stove, stove to sink, refrigerator to sink, and so on.

This is easily achieved in any L-shape or U-shape galley and is seen on almost every production or custom yacht. (A few designers use a straight-line galley to port or starboard. The set-up has some advantages for some boats, but it's inefficient motion management for the cook and, on a sailboat, it means that the entire galley is canted one way or the other when you're on a tack.)

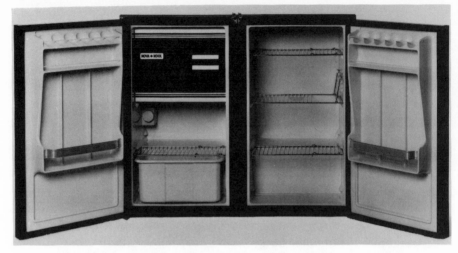

Nova Kool's double refrigerator runs on battery or shore power, and is designed for under-counter use. When shore power is available, the unit automatically switches from DC to AC. Box 80749, Burnaby, B.C., Canada V5H 3Y1.
NOVA KOOL

Only you can make your priority list of the things your galley must have no matter what, and things you will add if you can find space for them. The more experience you have had in cooking aboard, the better you can evaluate such "musts" because the criteria you use in a kitchen on land won't always apply in the galley.

For instance, most homes have dishwashers. Those sold for boats usually don't have built-in garbage grinders as household models do, so you have to do more rinsing and scraping. They use a lot of water, take up space you could be using for storage, and probably won't do the cleaning job you expect. A big freezer, on the other hand, might not be important to your kitchen because you shop daily and serve only fresh food. But on the boat, you want a large reserve of frozen foods in a big freezer.

A common mistake in production boats is to add amenities in places where they'll be dangerous or difficult to use. We once spent a week aboard a houseboat that had a microwave oven installed over a full-size household refrigerator. It was a long, overhead reach for me, and I'm five feet eight inches tall. To get hot casseroles in and out of this aerie was to invite spills and burns.

Aboard another boat, I couldn't get the oven door open without removing the coffee pot from the under-counter coffeemaker. Another had one of those built-in multipurpose appliances that uses one motor, mounted under the counter, to run a mixer, food processor, blender, and so forth. Because the motor was mounted in wasted space in a far corner of the counter, it was too far from the center of the work area to be used without a long, awkward reach.

On one bareboat in the Virgin Islands, I could reach the bottom of the icebox only by lying on the counter with head and shoulders inside the cavernous hole. I never got mad at the designer. I was laughing too hard. Galleys have to be laid out for the *people* who will use them.

The other thing to consider, if you're making major additions to the galley, is traffic flow. If crewmen can't move freely fore and aft while a temporary shelf is in place, or the kids can't get to the head when the refrigerator door is open, everyone feels crowded.

Storage and Counter Space

It is hard to find a production boat of any size, or a custom design by a professional architect, that doesn't make brilliant use of every inch of space. So, it's likely that your boat's storage areas are about as good as they can get. However, here are some thoughts on adding storage or work space.

- Counter space can be expanded by adding sink fill-ins, stove covers, or temporary shelving that pulls out, pops up, or unfolds from some hiding place.
- Ready-made storage modules are available in home-improvement stores. They include drawers that add on under counters, storage bins that slide out from under the sink, a spice shelf that drops down from under a cup-

Vinyl-coated wire kitchen accessories are convenient and durable in the galley.

THE WOODWORKERS' STORE

It looks like a drawer, but pulls out to provide extra galley counter space up to thirty-two inches long. The hardware, which is zinc-plated steel and which can support up to 176 pounds, costs about $120.

THE WOODWORKERS' STORE

board, and other items designed for kitchen use. Some have metal parts and will have a limited life in a salt-water boat.

• A ceramic cooktop, when cold, doubles as counter space.
• When stuffing items into unused spaces, make sure they don't interfere with needed air flow to refrigeration coils.
• If you have a top-access icebox or refrigerator, design the lid so it doubles as counter space or a cutting board.
• Often, wasted space can be found in the far end of a 90-degree corner. Cut a hole in the countertop, and access the space from the top. It's a good spot to drop in a wastebasket or an extra icebox.
• Don't forget to make at least one cupboard door wide enough to take big skillets and pots. Even in a miniature galley, full-size cookware is needed.
• Inexpensive plastic dish pans are clean, lightweight containers for all sorts of smaller items that are to be stowed in large compartments. Rubbermaid's Roughneck line of plastic containers is heavier duty, comes in many sizes, and has lids. Divide and conquer.
• Drawers and cupboard doors should have strong locks. When an entire set of cutlery shifts in rough seas, chaos can result.
• Often overlooked are unused spaces, however small and shallow, under a galley floor. When reflooring, add hatches over such areas.
• Also overlooked are the small, dead, air spaces between the sink and its cabinet. A shallow drawer or bin could be added in front of the sink, and a trough cut into the countertop in back of the sink. Both places make handy storage for pot scrapers and scrubbers.
• If you're having new cabinets made, make sure the carpenter measures all the way to the end of each drawer's travel. In a bank of thwartship drawers that follows the curve of the hull, the top drawer could be far deeper than the bottom one. In production boats, banks of drawers are often mass-produced in neat, uniform, dresserlike stacks sized to the shortest dimension. Space is wasted.

Choosing Galley Cookware

In the past decade, Americans have gone goofy for gourmet, which means a galaxy of new cookware for the cruising cook's choice. Some of the new housewares will solve old galley problems in brilliant new ways, but other new pots and pans are all wrong—often for reasons you least expect.

Stoves are another subject entirely (see p. 33) but we have to start there because so much depends on the kind of cooker(s) you have. Most of us use conventional pots because we have alcohol, kerosene, propane, or CNG (compressed natural gas) galley stoves. Increasing numbers of boat cooks are also adding a microwave and, with it, basic microwave cookware.

Another all-new technology is the conduction burner, not to be confused with the convection oven. A conduction cooktop stays cool while energy is conducted directly to the pan. Only ferrous pans—steel or iron, but not enameled steel or copper clad stainless—will work.

The Kinds of Cookware

Aluminum is cheap, strong, and an excellent conductor of heat. When I'm cruising without an oven, my big cast-aluminum skillet serves as a fryer, roaster, dutch oven, griddle, and omelet pan. Because I use it as an oven, and get it very hot, I didn't opt for a nonstick lining (which would be damaged by extreme heat). Aluminum has tiny pores to trap grease, so it "seasons" over time to a nonstick finish much as iron skillets do. Yet because of its superior heat-transfer properties, it is a far better stovetop oven.

Aluminum has its drawbacks. It reacts with acid foods, and it can warp or crack if abused. Never plunge a hot pan into cold water; don't store food in aluminum overnight. Heavy cast aluminum is best for long, slow cooking, and for keeping several pots hot at once while you shuffle them between two burners. Cheaper, thinner, stamped aluminum is fine for sauteeing and quick warm-ups.

My pressure cookers are aluminum because I also use them for stovetop baking if I don't have an oven aboard. Older pressure cookers are heavier, thicker, cast aluminum. Newer models are thinner, stamped aluminum. If you can find an old pressure cooker in a thrift shop, grab it unless it's an off brand for which you can no longer find parts and gaskets. Stovetop baking techniques are covered fully in my book *Cooking on the Go* (Hearst Marine Books).

Copper. Because it's the best heat conductor of any cookware metals, copper is favored by professional chefs. In salt water, it's a bother to keep clean, and it's even worse if the pan has iron handles. Between rust, corrosion, and galvanic action, you have a tiger by the tail in a copper pot. Too, copper pans need relining periodically, and that's expensive.

One piece that you may find worth carrying is an unlined copper beating bowl. Because whipping cream or egg whites tend to "climb" the sides of the bowl, you can get very airy froths using only a whisk.

A time-honored method for cleaning copper is to dip a cut lemon in salt, scrub the copper, let stand a few minutes, then rinse well with fresh water, and dry.

If you use copper pans, coddle them. Copper melts at 450 degrees, so take care not to overheat it and don't let pans boil dry. Use wooden utensils to keep from damaging pan linings, which may be stainless steel, tin, nickel or, sometimes, silver.

Iron and steel. All ferrous metals are slow to spread heat, so they are often a poor choice for the often-cramped spaces of a galley. Grandma's iron skillet was perfect for use on the old wood range and, placed over a flame that is only two to three inches in diameter, steel pans can develop hot spots in the center.

Ironware is fine for oven baking, and for use atop a large cook surface such as a diesel potburner-type galley stove, a charcoal brazier, large gas or electric burner, or a wood or coal stove. While it's a poor choice for a stovetop oven, iron is a good oven in a beach fire when surrounded and topped with hot coals.

Iron is heavy and it rusts, so I don't like to carry it aboard, but many cooks won't be separated from their iron skillets because cast iron "seasons" to a natural, nonstick finish. When the pan is new, oil it with vegetable oil or shortening and heat it in a 350-degree oven for an hour. Or, if the pan had been silicone-treated at the factory, grease it lightly and bake at 250 degrees for thirty minutes. This initial treatment seals fat in the pores, giving the pan a nonstick surface. If rust develops, or if foods stick badly, reseason according to the first method.

Enameled ironware looks good in stove-to-table use, but it can get chipped in knock-about galley use. In time the enamel darkens and there is little you can do to lighten it. Bleach and abrasives make matters worse. If you choose enameled ware, do so knowing you will have to coddle it.

Stainless steel is sturdy, good-looking, and it doesn't react with foods. Its heat transfer is poor, but many manufacturers add layers of other metals, such as aluminum or copper, for even heating.

I like Lifetime Stainless (it's sold through home-party plans) because it's all stainless outside with other metals sealed in the very thick, heat-retaining bottom. It's so thick, and so well lidded, that cooking continues for up to ten minutes after the pan is taken off the heat—a real plus when you're shuffling several pans between two burners.

Any sandwich-core pan (copper or aluminum between two layers of stainless steel) can be damaged from quick temperature changes, such as putting a refrigerated pan over a hot burner or cooling a hot pan in cold water. I once boiled potatoes dry in a very expensive cored pot, and it delaminated. My Lifetime has stood up to similar accidents for thirty years, so I recommend it.

Any steel that is 11½ percent chrome can be called stainless, but I've had rust problems with cheaper grades—especially in salt-water cruising. Look for the designation 18/8 or higher. This stands for 18 percent chromium and 8 percent nickel.

Black steel. Professional cooks prefer black steel for baking breads and pastries. Because black steel pans work at oven temperatures 15–20 degrees cooler than shiny pans, they'll save fuel in the galley. However, this steel rusts and the tender surface scratches easily.

Tinned steel, too, can rust, scratch, and react with foods. If you use a tinned-steel pudding mold, remove the pudding immediately after cooking or a tinny taste may taint the food.

T-Fal's raven-black Royale cookware is porcelain clad. Ultrabase exterior is triple thick; Ultra-T-Plus interior eliminates sticking, cleanup, and scratching. The company makes cookware in many styles and colors.
TEFAL APPLIANCES

New plastic bakeware can be used both in the microwave and in conventional ovens below 400 degrees. Higher-temperature plastics are on the horizon. Sets stack for stowage, and weight is a fraction of that of metal cookware.
RUBBERMAID

Nonstick finishes. My favorites are Tefal and the new Silverstone Supra. Although the new coatings are more durable than the old Teflon, they shouldn't be abused by overheating and abrasion. Slip each piece into an old pillowcase or other protector before nesting pans in your lockers; use only nonmetal utensils.

Plastics and paper. Many new heatproof plastics are on the market. Some are made just for microwaving; others can be used in an oven below 400 degrees or so. Plastics eventually scratch, stain, and absorb flavors but are still preferable to glass for microwaving aboard because they are lightweight and unbreakable. Look for new, ultrahigh-temperature plastics to be available in the future. They will be usable in conventional ovens.

Pottery, ceramic, porcelain, glass, earthenware. One of my cruising friends dotes on clay-pot cooking, and doesn't mind the extra time it takes to wrap and stow her clayware where it won't get broken. Another friend won't sail without his bean pot. But, unless you have a special love for any of these breakables and are willing to take the time to care for them, they're best left on shore.

Some Galley Favorites

Only you can decide how many pots you need in what metals, coatings, and sizes. Here are some of my most faithful cooking aids.

- *Hackman Steamer.* This pot from Finland consists of a roomy stockpot, a double boiler, and a spacious steamer insert. An entire meal can be cooked on one burner. It's a shiny, fine-grade stainless, so it goes from stove to table. Sold in cooking specialty shops and catalogs.
- *Pressure cooker.* Mine is four quarts, large enough to make soups and stews for a crew of up to six. For larger crews, get a six- or eight-quart pressure pan. In many instances (cooking ten potatoes, for example) the pressure cooker is faster than a microwave oven. If you'll be using it nonpressured, e.g., for stovetop baking, get aluminum. Otherwise, stainless steel is best.

30

Dual-purpose appliances are lifesavers for the galley cook. Tefal's Flip-Over toaster is also a broiler.
TEFAL APPLIANCES

- *Stainless-steel folding stovetop toaster.* Ordinary steel toasters rust out too quickly; rigid models take up too much room in storage. Find them in marine and camp-supply catalogs.
- *Cheap nonstick skillets.* I have three sizes, and like them as well as any $150 sauté pans. In time, despite one's best efforts, the coatings degrade, so I buy inexpensive pans and replace them as necessary.
- *Thermos bottles.* They're as important as any pans in my galley. With boiling water always on hand, you don't have to light the stove to make instant coffee or a cup of tea. If I'm short of burners, I can make soup, gravy, or a sauce ahead of time and keep it serving-hot in a thermos. I like wide-mouth models because they can be

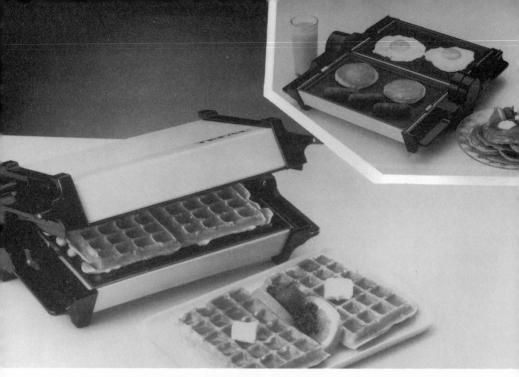

Three appliances in one, Tefal's waffle maker can be
clipped open and used as a griddle, or closed with its
sandwich plates in place to make hot sandwiches.
TEFAL APPLIANCES

Tabletop appliances like this Gourmet Party Set can be
used at the center of the table. Everyone gathers around
to make their own raclette, fajitas, or mixed grill.
TEFAL APPLIANCES

used for chunky foods as well as for hot liquids, and
stainless-steel bottles because they are unbreakable.

- *Boilable bags.* Heatproof plastic bags (Reynolds Roast-
ing Bags, or bags sold for use with home food sealers)
are ideal for leftovers. To rewarm, just place in simmering water. You'll have no pots to wash.

Baking Without an Oven

Tinny stovetop ovens can be found in camp stores, but they rust,
take up too much room in storage, and are very hard to keep up
to baking temperature—especially on cold or windy days.

In my book *Cooking on the Go*, which can be ordered from
(800)866-2326, I describe four stovetop cooking methods. Two
are "direct," in which the product bakes directly on the hot surface of the pan. Two others are "indirect" because you put the
dough or batter in a pan which is then placed inside another. The
indirect method may take longer, but when you're finished, the
"oven" itself is still clean.

Tip: Buy your dutch oven and cake and pie pans all on the
same shopping trip, to make sure the smaller pans will fit inside
the large one.

Cooktops

For the galley cook, few choices are more important, and more
confusing, than the stove or cooktop. Today's cook has to look far
beyond the old decision of gas versus electric, kerosene, or alcohol. The remodeler has to consider plumbing, wiring, gimbals,
rails, and cutout size. And, if a downdraft cooktop is involved, a
complicated vent formula must be figured in.

Where once a galley chef would settle for the best compromise, the choice now will probably be for multiple stoves—for
example, a propane cooktop plus self-cleaning electric oven and

By combining components, it's possible to have a very versatile cooktop incorporating downdraft grilling with gas, electric, or induction burners. MODERN MAID

a microwave oven. Or, a downdraft cooktop and grill plus a combination microwave-convection oven.

There are too many good, new technologies for the cook to settle for just one cooker.

What's New in Marine Stoves

CNG (compressed natural gas) made an initial splash as a safe fuel, but its high cost and strictly localized availability were problems for many boat owners. However, CNG stoves, as well as a large choice of pressurized and unpressurized alcohol and kerosene cookers, combination electric-alcohol burners, and propane stoves, are offered by leading marine stove makers such as Plastimo, Origo Division of Dometic, Kenyon, and TASCO.

The biggest sellers among galley stoves are propane for cruising boats, and electric for most power boats and for those sailors who do most of their cooking dockside. Many "muscle" boats have nothing but a microwave.

Diesel and woodburning stoves are still popular too, especially in cold waters Down East and in the Pacific Northwest. They are the most practical and salty of boat stoves in waters where their warming heat is welcome in a chilly cabin. Most of us, however, boat in more temperate climates, and prefer a stove that doesn't create such an intense reservoir of heat.

We once spent two weeks with our friends Chris and Chuck Grey who had built and outfitted their boat in Washington state, brought her down the coast and through the Panama Canal, and into the Bay Islands. We joined them in Honduras and sailed with them to Cozumel.

This was not the Grey's first boat, and they had furnished this troller exactingly and in keeping with their years of long-distance cruising experience. Chris's galley was a gleaming gem—clean, lean, absolutely perfect.

I immediately fell in love with her diesel pot burner stove, the first I'd seen. Like Grandma's old, black iron cookstove, it took a while to get hot but when it got going it was enough stove to cook a wedding feast. Quick-cook items could be placed directly over the burners; other foods simmered over portions of the cast-iron top that were not directly over the fire.

There were places where you could coddle a sauce, warm a stack of plates, sizzle a stir fry, or tuck a yeast loaf to rise. The oven was a dream. And there was always enough residual heat after a meal to dry the dish towels and to keep the kettle warm for a late cup of tea.

Chris and I had to agree that such a stove was just too hot for the tropics but I can see why they are so popular in Maine, British Columbia, England, and Holland. One brand is Dickinson Manufacturing Co. Ltd., 407-204 Cayer St., Coquitam, B.C., Canada V3K 5B1. Hot-water baseboard heaters can be run off larger Dickinson models. Other suppliers include Washington Stove Works, P.O. Box 687, Everett, WA 98206 and Shipmate Stove, Richmond Ring Co., Souderton, PA 18964.

Force 10 Marine Ltd., 23080 Hamilton Rd., Richmond, B.C., Canada V6V 1C9 offers a stellar selection of gas and oil marine ranges in many sizes and styles including its famous "disappearing" door models. Construction is stainless steel, bronze, and brass throughout. The company also sells barbecues, lanterns, heaters, and conversion units to turn alcohol burners into diesel or kerosene burners.

With the popularity of nonpressurized units, alcohol stoves have made a comeback, although alcohol remains an inefficient, costly fuel. Origo, for one, offers a large choice of alcohol and combination alcohol-electric cooktops, an alcohol stove with oven, and an alcohol oven that takes no more space than a microwave.

Household Cooktops

There are disadvantages to having a nonmarine stove in your galley. It probably can't be gimballed, and it may rust out more quickly. Safety may also be a problem unless the stove and its installation meet strict marine standards. Some household gas stoves cannot be lit without power to the electronic ignition. On others, top burners can be lit manually but the oven cannot.

Still, as yachts become bigger and more luxurious, with larger generators designed to provide full-time household power, more cooks are choosing to do some, and perhaps all, of their cooking with household appliances. The first downdraft stove, and the first ceramic cooktop I ever saw were on boats, not in kitchens.

Configuration. This is the easy part, because cooktops come in an almost limitless choice of styles and sizes. Two, three, or four burners are spread out or clustered together, with controls located to the right, left, or center.

If you have to fit an existing opening in the counter, no problem. If you want to design a new cooktop of any size, the sky's the limit. It's possible now to find controls designed for the left-handed cook, or for island installation in which a stove could be used from either side. Many of the new knobs and indicators are designed to be used or read from either direction.

Because many two-burner cooktops are available, you can combine modules to design a large, restaurant-style galley. Start with, say, two propane burners at one end, then a downdraft grill and a griddle in the center, and a ceramic cooktop on the other side. Or, place a downdraft grill at one end of the counter where

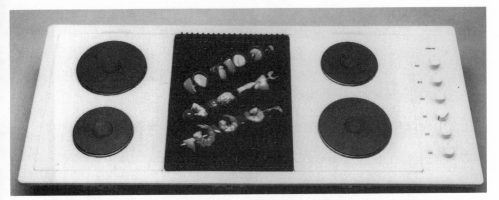

The marketplace now offers an almost endless choice of cooktops in all sizes, shapes, and cooking combinations. This one (above), by Dacor, incorporates four solid elements and a barbecue. Also by Dacor (below) is this two-element electric cooktop with barbecue module. DACOR

the barbecue chef can work, and four burners at the other end of the counter to provide a work center for the rest of the meal.

Today's trend in kitchens is the "team" approach. Galleys, too, are becoming larger, more a part of the "family room," and more welcoming to the entire crew.

The New Burners. Traditional gas grate-type burners are still popular. There is also the hob grate, which fits over two or more

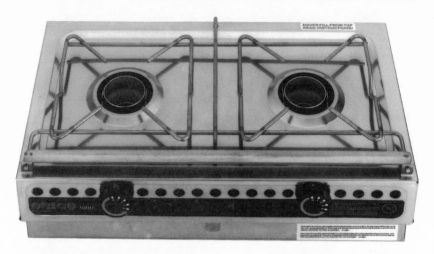

Origo's alcohol stove features a hob type grate, on which one large, or two or three smaller, pots can be arranged. Hobs are also being seen now on larger household gas stoves which are favored by some galley cooks. ORIGO

gas burners, allowing the cook to use several pots at once. It's a good option for the space-pinched galley cook who wants to steam vegetables at the back of the hob, sauté another dish over the front burner, and simmer sauces in the space between. Electric burners are available in both coil, and sealed solid, styles.

Glass Cooktops. Early glass cooktops weren't as quick or as cleanable as promised, but ceramics are again hot news and they are newly practical for the galley because they serve as flat, clean counter space when cool. Withstanding temperatures to 1300 degrees without expanding or contracting, the new ceramics don't warp and are very hard to break. Yellowing has been eliminated and, because elements are placed closer to the glass, more heat is achieved with less wattage.

Ceramics are nonporous, so they form an excellent bond with any type pots and they are easy to clean. Most are conventional, radiant heat but there are two new technologies to consider.

In one new method, induction cooking, energy is transferred directly from power coils through the ceramic cooktop, and into (ferrous) pots. The stove itself stays cool. Only iron and stainless steel pans can be used; copper and aluminum do not react with this magnetic energy.

Response is instantaneous, much like that of gas, but much quicker and hotter. It's ideal for stir frying and other techniques favored by cooks who, until now, shunned electric cooking because of its slow heat-cool reaction. Sears's induction burners turn off automatically one minute after a pan is removed. Temperatures are infinitely controllable, from very low (for melting chocolate) to very quick (for stir frying). One induction burner is a definite plus for any galley where electricity is available even part of the time.

Another new technology, quartz halogen burners which were brought to the United States from Britain by Amana, produce instant heat and light through vacuum-sealed quartz glass tubes filled with halogen gas. The burner is surrounded by a resistance coil, to distribute heat more evenly.

One of the old complaints about ceramic cooktops has been that they look the same hot or cold. Accidents and burns can result when something or someone touches a hot cooktop that looks cool. Amana's InstaGlow four-element cooktop, which features one or two quartz-halogen burners and two or three resistance elements, glows to show that a burner is on.

The news in gas-burner technology is the sealed Sourdillion burner which has a cast-iron head with drilled ports. The flame is shorter, more intense, and said to be up to 30 percent more efficient. Since no extra air is needed for combustion, burners are sealed to the cooktop so spills can't get under the catch cups.

Sears offers a cooktop model, and a Sourdillion stove with self-cleaning oven. Both reignite automatically if the flame is blown out. Ignition is by individual electrode, so the flame can be started at any valve setting—you no longer have to start with a burst of flame as with other gas burners.

Downdrafts. Ever since they were introduced twenty years ago, downdraft cookers have been the delight of cooks who like to grill meat and fish without having to light a barbecue on deck. Downdrafts are clean, quick, trendy, and an excellent selling point when you put the boat up for sale.

Most major stove manufacturers offer at least one downdraft

Downdraft grills are available alone, in cooktops that also have burners, in complete stoves, and separately. Today's yacht can have a completely customized stove utilizing many types of burners. JENN-AIR

stove or cooktop. GE's five-hundred-cfm blower can be vented up to one hundred feet, subtracting distance for obstacles such as bends, corners, and caps according to a formula provided by the manufacturer.

Jenn-Air, which uses a three-hundred-cfm blower and which offers both gas and electric downdraft grills, has models that can be used with runs up to sixty feet. The company's ducting formula calls for, for example, deducting five feet from the allowable length for each six-inch, 90-degree elbow in six-inch round ducting. The run will be different for each boat, depending on how many turns and caps are involved.

Key to the new Jenn-Air models is a larger blower motor with a restrictor ring that provides proper air movement for duct runs of up to thirty feet without pulling so much air that cooking is affected adversely. This restrictor ring can be reached from the top of the cooktop, and snapped out without tools. Internally vented downdrafts, which depend on a filtering system, are also available.

Modern Maid division of Caloric Corporation, a Raytheon company, also offers a gas downdraft. Everything comes apart for easy cleaning. Even the control panel can be put into a dishwasher. The 120V vent system can be run up to twenty-six feet.

Microwaves. Aboard any boat that has electricity available even part of the time, it is more tempting than ever to incorporate a microwave. MWs come in many sizes and types, from a tiny warm-up oven to large, completely automatic ovens. Many small luxury boats now come from the factory with no other stove— and many boatmen find the MW does everything from making coffee to rewarming dishes brought from home, deli, caterer, or take-out restaurant.

The microwave has become so much a part of today's cooking scene, it's almost an essential in the galley. Unless you have full-time 110V power, get one of the simpler models. More sophisticated types, with built-in clock and programming, have to be reset every time power is restored. In a small galley where you have no room for a conventional oven, a combination microwave-convection oven is a good choice.

Making Your Choice

Independence. Gas stoves are no longer feared as they once were because new sniffers, automatic solenoid fuel shut-offs, automatic lighting, and other safeguards make them a safer alternative. Gas is a hot, quick, quiet, familiar fuel.

For the long-distance cruiser, such stoves may mean difficulties with refills. I've known sailors who had to haul tanks long distances by bus or taxi for refilling, or send tanks back to "civilization" by freight boat. Too, several different valves are used worldwide, so you have to carry a good choice to make sure you have one that is compatible with the refill station's valve.

Pressure kerosene stoves remain a good choice for the cruiser in the most remote areas because kerosene is available almost everywhere. It is hot, quick cooking, and cheap. On the minus side, some paraffin stoves require priming with costly alcohol, and they can be smoky and cranky.

Diesel fuel can be burned in most pressure kerosene stoves. Diesel pot-burner stoves are a good choice for the boat that sails cold climates but they're very hot to use in the tropics. Like wood and coal stoves, such stoves have one big cooktop which has hot spots and warm spots so you can shuffle pots among them for every task from sautéing to simmering.

Coastal cruisers often choose a combination alcohol-electric cooktop. When little cooking is done at anchor or underway, alcohol is a good alternative to running a generator. And, it uses the same burners so it's space efficient. But alcohol is an eye-smarting, expensive, inefficient fuel that gives fewer BTU's per gallon and per dollar than any other.

Although some boatmen consider alcohol a safer fuel because its flames can be extinguished with water, remember that the period of danger—that is, anytime a flame is burning in your boat—is longer with alcohol to produce any given meal because it heats so much more slowly than other fuels. And, if you splash water on a big pool of burning alcohol, you just spread the fire around.

Special Pots. Before making a final decision on stoves and fuels, consider whether you'll have to carry special cookware.

You'll need nonmetal cookware for the microwave. Only iron or stainless-steel cookware can be used with induction cooking. Glass, aluminum, copper clad, and porcelainized steel pots do not react with this energy. While newer ceramic cooktops can be used with both metal and glass cookware, bottoms should be as smooth and flat as possible; rounded or contoured bottoms don't make good contact with the glass.

Grills. Not all grill inserts are downdrafts. Some are just grills (which may euphemistically be called "updrafts"). Before introducing any grill to the galley, make sure you have a hood and adequate venting to deal with the spatters, heat, steam, and mess.

Cleanability. Some cooktops are completely sealed; some allow boilovers to leak through. Some break down into components which can be placed in a dishwasher or taken out on deck for serious scrubbing.

Nautical or neutral themes are available in melamine tableware with nonskids backs. YACHTING TABLEWARE

Cost. The simplest, four-burner kitchen-type cooktops sell for about $200; two-burner modules for as little as $100. A radiant cooktop is $600 or less, $50 more for each quartz-halogen element. Downdraft modules are about $500. Sears's four-burner induction cooktop is $700 for the 30″ and $750 for the 36″ model. Good, stainless-steel marine stoves sell for double and triple the price of similarly sized stoves sold for household or recreational vehicle use. Some sailors find it cheaper to buy RV stoves and replace them as they rust out.

Safety. All stoves can be dangerous. They should be installed according to marine wiring and gas plumbing standards, and equipped with whatever extra safeguards you can find or devise (e.g., fireproof tiles around the stove, automatic gas shut-offs, gimbals, fiddles, pot clamps).

Although I've written at great length here about household stoves in addition to marine stoves, it should be obvious that a wet galley in a heaving boat is not the place for an electric stove with a glass-smooth cooking surface. It must be remembered that boats move, sometimes violently.

I've seen, firsthand, only a few boats that have had stove fires. One burned to the waterline because curtains near the stove caught fire while children made popcorn. Another had to be abandoned, and was a total loss, because a single-hander left something cooking down below and went on deck. Another burned because a leak in a pressure alcohol line had been mended with electrical tape!

Among those stoves that are not best for boat use are pressure gasoline campstoves, and portable gas stoves which use small propane or butane cylinders. The cylinders themselves can rust through quickly, and leak.

Still, it's the chef, not the stove, that usually makes the safety difference.

Other Galley Equipment

Central vacuum systems. Growing in popularity in homes, central vacuum systems are standard equipment on most top-of-the-line recreational vehicles. Now Origo has designed one for marine use. The 1000W motor stows below decks in any 16″ × 20″ × 8″ spot. When the cleaning hose is attached, a micro-switch automatically turns on the vacuum. Extension tubes, hoses, and attachments come with the set. Origo Division, 1121 Lewis Ave., Sarasota, FL 34237.

Crisper. This breadbox-size appliance has a heating strip that keeps crackers and cookies crisp. Store dry items—snacks, cereals, grains—in it. It's available from Hammacher Schlemmer catalogs and stores.

Dishwasher. Husqvarna's Swedish-made countertop dishwasher is available through Berg Corp., 30 Overlook Terrace, Roslyn Hts., NY 11577. All stainless steel, it can be built-in or portable, and has electric water preheat.

General Electric's compact Spacemaker line of appliances includes a trash compactor, small refrigerators, radio-TV, coffeemaker, toaster, and a tiny refrigerator-icemaker combo.

Long a galley favorite, the Brisker uses low heat to keep cereals and crackers crisp. HAMMACHER SCHLEMMER

This Swedish-made dishwasher is all stainless steel, fits very small space.
BERG CORPORATION

Self-stowing knife sets have many advantages for the galley. Holder can be screwed to a bulkhead or left in a drawer. Knives are held securely underway. Each sheath has a built-in sharpener; knife is automatically honed each time it is pulled out.
WILKINSON SWORD

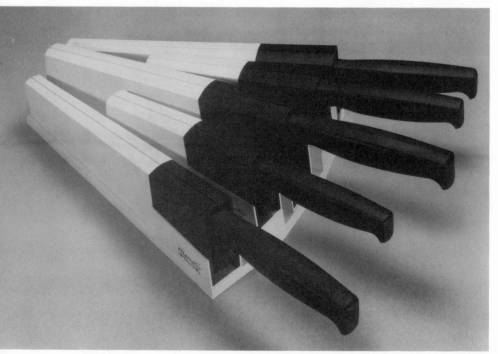

Portable electric coolers make ideal "extras" to use around the boat on deck, on the flybridge, and below. Stash bait and fish in separate coolers, to keep odors away from foods. Ice canned drinks in another cooler on deck, to keep traffic out of the galley. Where coolers can also double as seats, so much the better. Some 12V coolers also have a heat setting, and can be used to warm foods.
COLEMAN

47

Small-size dish drainers
are ideal for quick clean-
ups in the galley.
RUBBERMAID

This European washer-
dryer combination can be
set to do a complete laundry, from wash through a
choice of dry cycles.
BERG CORPORATION

Downsize household appliances, including GE's Spacemaker line, are ideal for yacht use. Spacemakers include under-counter appliances and such items as a combination refrigerator-icemaker and a 12-inch-wide compactor that fits under the sink.

GENERAL ELECTRIC

Norcold division of Stolle Corp., 1501 Michigan St., Sidney, OH 45365 makes a full line of AC-DC refrigerators and an icemaker.

Origo, a division of Dometic, offers a 12V refrigerator, and two 115V icemakers. Designed for the marine trade, they are coated for corrosion resistance.

Tailgater is a 12V version of Waring's time-proven blender. It's available through 12V suppliers and through stores that sell Waring blenders.

T-Fal is one of the best, toughest, and most reliable nonsticks. The company makes complete sets of nonstop cookware and baking ware, as well as a line of compact, versatile appliances. T-Fal Corporation, 208 Passaic Ave., Fairfield, NJ 07006.

Washer-dryer. A completely automatic, compact, Italian-made washer-dryer with five cycles is available from Berg Corp., address above. It includes such features as cool-down dry, liquid bleach and softener dispensers, and stainless-steel tub and drum. It holds up to twelve pounds for wash only, eight pounds washdry, and consumes no more than thirty gallons of water.

Water heaters. A line of compact, 110/220V water heaters in capacities of six, ten, twelve, and twenty gallons is available through Daimen Corp., 449 N. Pennsylvania Ave., Morrisville, PA 19067. Where water conservation is important, it's sometimes better to install several small heaters around the boat rather than one large heater that is a long distance from the farthest outlet. When water must be run for a long time while waiting for hot water to arrive, many quarts are wasted.

Even less water waste occurs when a tankless water heater is installed at each hot-water faucet. The advantage to tanks is that they hold heat for hours after the power (or engine) is off; tankless heaters require ignition (generator or flame) to operate. Household 110V models are available through home-plumbing suppliers. Tankless water heaters that operate on propane, butane, or CNG are available from Wolter Systems, 1100 Harrison Ave., Cincinnati, OH 45214 and through Daimen Corporation.

Chapter 3

~~~~~~

BEDDING AND LINENS

~~~~~~

The bed in your master stateroom may be built from $2000 worth of solid teak and have a $600 mattress, but what your eye sees first as you enter the stateroom is probably a set of bed linens that cost $200 or less. Few decorating statements in your boat are more important to a dashing decor, as well as to comfort and convenience, than your choice of bed coverings.

Most boat owners need two types of bedding, one for those beds that are full-time beds, and another for making up convertible beds that during the day serve as sofas, dinettes, or cockpit seats. The more difficult the bedmaking situation, especially in beds that must be made up each night and stowed each morning, the more important it is to have the right linens—even if they must be custom-made.

The reason is simple. If your bed is shaped like a trapezoid, is the size of an atoll, and has to be turned each night from a chart table into a bunk, the job will be much easier if you use linens that were designed for the shape and thickness of the mattress. Custom linens can also be equipped with whatever elastic, grippers, hook-loop, and drawstrings will make it easiest to get the linens on the bed each night and which will keep them there through whatever tossings and thrashings occur.

Exotic animal prints, from ocelet to zebra, are featured in the Native Sun line from Nautical Image. The company custom creates linens to fit any size bunk. NAUTICAL IMAGE

Although I made custom bed coverings for our own boat, I've had many wretched nights on bareboats where we were given a stack of flat sheets and left to our own devices. Some barely covered the mattress, let alone tucked in.

Once, in Scotland, we were issued sleeping bags that were long enough to cover Gordon to his waist and me only to mid-chest. We nearly froze, and the next morning went to an inn where we begged to rent a few blankets for a week. Now we carry our own Travasak (see below) when bareboating.

A leading creator of marine linens is Susan Schuler, whose Nautical Image Inc. grosses six figures annually by selling her unique Cinch system-bedding, monogrammed bed and bath linens, and a full range of duvets, neckrolls, shams, dust covers, robes, and other accessories.

Working only with fine fabrics including 280-count-weave Egyptian cottons and percale blends, and real suedes, downs, silks, and cashmeres, Schuler sells made-to-order sizes in the newest styles, all tailored to the shape of the berth and fitted with special snaps and other devices to keep them taut and in place. Once fitted and knotted, the drawstring can be left in place during laundering. It usually doesn't need readjusting.

For information about Nautical Image, call (800)547-4433. Custom linen specialists also include Sleep at Sea, 11 Princeton, Irvine, CA 92720; and G&T Industries, 7126 Henry G Lane, Maryville, TN 37801.

A prestige presence in New York since the 1920's, Léron continues to maintain its stringent standards in custom linens in Belgian linen, French and Italian silks, and 300-count Egyptian cotton. Léron works to order, sending pieces to France, Italy, Switzerland, or Portugal for hand embroidery or appliqué. The company also does table and bath linens, and personal lingerie. If you are budgeting for the very highest quality and price, write Léron at 750 Madison Ave., New York, NY 11021 and they'll send a sales representative to meet with you or your yacht decorator.

Alternative Sleeping Systems

Sleeping bags have become silky sophisticates, combining the satiny feel of the best percales with the practicality of an all-purpose bed cover that can be rolled up and stowed during the day. In addition to conventional sleeping bags, there are multilayer sleeping sacks as well as complete systems that incorporate their own mattress.

The advantages are many. For one thing, some boat bunks can't be made up with conventional sheets because there is no way to secure bottom sheets or to tuck in top sheets and blankets. Picture, for instance, a banquette that folds out to form a double bed but which doesn't have separate cushions to form a mattress. Or, on power boats, fore-and-aft seats that fold flat to create single bunks.

Marine vinyl upholstery is sticky hot, and so slippery that bedding goes askew within minutes after bedtime. When that vinyl is not only slippery but affords no place to tuck in a bottom sheet, a sleeping bag is the only way to surround the sleeper securely and to insulate his skin from the vinyl.

Sleeping bags, sacks, and systems are usually the best choice for convertible beds because they can quickly be brandished across the bed each night. They don't come unscrambled because they surround the body like an envelope. In the morning, just roll them up and stuff them in a locker.

One of the best such systems is Travasak from Travamerica, 26041 Pala, Mission Viejo, CA 92692, telephone (714)587-8440. I first met company president Tim Jones when he was a young entrepreneur selling to the RV market. Yachtsmen began ordering Travasak, and Jones began showing at boat shows.

From the beginning, he has produced only the finest quality bed sacks, using the best materials and incorporating features that ordinary sleeping bags do not offer. The bag itself has a heavy side, to place on top on cold nights, and a thinner side to sleep under in summer.

The sacks are lined with percale sheets which attach, full length, with hook-and-loop fasteners. Sheets stay put while you sleep, yet can easily be removed for laundering. Each side of the

Travasack's complete sleeping system has full-length hook-and-loop fasteners which allow easy removal of sheets on laundry day. TRAVASACK

sack has its own self-lubricating, rustproof zipper, and the bottom can also be unzipped. Travasak is sold in single and double sizes in four colors, and each comes with a tote sack. Also available are color-coordinated pillow shams, additional percale liners, and a dust ruffle.

The bag itself is percale filled with Quallofil; it can be laundered like a comforter. Zipped closed, it can also be used as a comforter atop conventional bedding. In use, Travasak looks, feels, and sleeps like a real home-made bed.

Sof-Berth is also a complete bedding system that begins with an expanse of hand washable "egg crate" foam mattress padding encased in a removable percale envelope. It includes a quilted pad, winter or summer blanket, and a unique, pleated top sheet. The system comes in its own duffel bag; matching shams can be ordered.

Sof-Berth is made to measure, according to dimensions you supply. Because of its sculptured foam core, it is cushy enough to use on the deck or beach if you run out of bunks. It's ideal for use atop lumpy or hard beds, and on convertible seats that present uncomfortable seams, welting, and crevices.

Coleman's BedRoll system is a double sleeping bag with zip-out percale sheets. It's thicker on one side for cold nights; on hot nights, sleep under the "summer" side.

L. L. Bean's Kennebec sleeping bags also use thin and thick sides. The bags are made of 100 percent nylon taffeta lined with a cotton-poly-nylon blend and insulated with DuPont Quallofil. Two-way nylon zippers allow two bags to be zipped together. Each bag comes with a coated nylon stuff sack.

Cabela's makes an Adam and Eve sleeping bag with a cotton duck outer shell that grips better than taffetas do, especially when placed on a plastic air mattress or vinyl upholstery. There's a pocket for inserting the air mattress if you like, and pillows that attach with Velcro. The 72" × 80" double can zip apart to create two 36" singles.

About Foam Mattresses

Rarely will a yacht bed have a mattress other than one made from man-made foam. It's comfortable, forgiving, and much lighter in weight than a natural foam rubber or innerspring mattress. Because mattresses should be turned very often for venting, and sometimes have to be raised repeatedly during the day to get into stowage areas under the bed, lightness is an important feature.

Foam mattresses and cushions break down, gradually losing their resiliency. When replacing them, go to a good foam supplier and ask about the many densities available. Thickness is not the only determinant. You may be able to get as much comfort from a thinner, firmer mattress than from a thick, low-density foam that lets your bones sink straight to the deck.

Some boat owners buy two thin mattresses, a firmer foam for the bottom and one with more "give" on top, and cement them together to form one mattress. In cuddy cabins where headroom is very limited, strive to get the most cushioning comfort in the thinnest mattress. Too, open-cell foam tends to hold water, which is a problem in boats with heavy condensation. You may want to sandwich the foam of your choice between thin outer layers of closed-cell foam, which will shed, not absorb, condensation that gathers on the plywood platform.

One foam specialist I contacted offered two dozen different foams in Super Soft, Soft, Medium Soft, Medium Economy, Firm, Extra Firm, Super Firm, and Extra Firm Loaded, in white and colors. Bolsters and pillows are also available in stock sizes. Look in the telephone yellow pages under Upholsterers or Mattresses, Custom.

Some additional tips:

- Scotchgarding bedspreads is a good investment. Retreat after dry cleaning.
- When several seat cushions are put together to form a bunk, uncomfortable lines and lumps are created by the cording in the upholstery. Invest in good mattress pads.
- When ordering a custom mattress, indicate the measurements of the finished piece, not the cut size of the foam itself. The foam shrinks an inch or more in each dimension as it is compressed into the ticking.
- Turn boat mattresses each time you change beds. Because they sit on a solid plywood base they get less air circulation than a mattress-boxspring-frame setup at home. Regularly spray the base with a household disinfectant, to kill mildew spores.
- Unusual foam, air, and self-inflating pillows and mattresses are offered by Basic Designs, 5815 Bennett Valley Rd., Santa Rosa, CA 95404.
- Wool fleece mattress pads are hospital proven. Used under the bottom sheet, a lambswool mattress pad is warmer in cool weather and cool in summer. Wool, unlike other fabrics, can also keep you warm when wet—

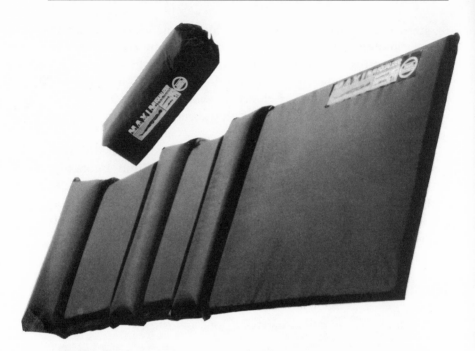

Self-inflating mattresses and pillows stow compactly, yet provide comfortable sleeping on deck or atop convertible seats. BASIC DESIGNS INC.

a plus in a damp boat. Eddie Bauer, (800) 426-8020 (ask for free catalog) offers washable wool mattress pads in many sizes, and matching wool pillow covers.
• If clean linens have been stowed for long periods, launder them again before laying up the boat. Spontaneous stains develop.
• If your boat manufacturer sells a linen package, it may be the best choice because the colors and fit will be right on target. Wellcraft Marine and Bluewater are among boat builders that offer custom linens.
• To make a temporary quick fit for a vee berth, bring together two sides of a flat sheet, tie a knot, and draw the sheet over the narrow side of the vee. Tuck in remaining edges.
• When buying sheets, get plenty of extra matching pillow-

cases and shams. In steamy weather, fresh pillowcases will give the bed a crisp, clean feel even if you're cruising in areas where you aren't able to launder the sheets as often as you'd like. Shams can be filled with extra blankets, jackets, or other bulky items that are a stowage problem, and used as throw pillows during the day.

- Buy or sew a stuff sack to hold each sleeping bag. The sleeping bag will stow more compactly and stay cleaner.
- You may not need custom sheets. Odd-size sheets which aren't found in department stores are sold through the Sears or J. C. Penney's catalogs, and by the Vermont Country Store, P.O. Box 3000, Manchester Ctr., VT 05255. Included are fitted and flat bunk sheets, cots, California kings, duplexes, three-quarter beds, sofabeds, and extra-longs, some of them in flannels as well as percales. Know your beds' exact dimensions. You may find readymade sheet sets that fit.

Chapter 4

~~~~~~

USE YOUR HEAD

~~~~~~

Although there will always be sailors who insist that the wooden bucket cannot be improved upon, yacht bathrooms have come into the glamour age. Yet you and your decorator must remember that the needs of the vessel come first.

These needs are many, and they are inescapable. You must provide your own water supply, water pressure, water heating, a drainage system that may require a series of pumps, sewage disposal and/or sewage treatment, and maintenance of the entire lash-up. In addition, you must provide safe venting for sewer gases, and keep a very complicated plumbing system free of clogs, odors, and algae.

In planning the head(s) you also have to consider size, space, weight, and center of gravity. If you want a bathtub or big spa, decks may need extensive reinforcement to support the added weight. Your boat has to be protected against the massive mildew problems that will be created if you don't vent the head adequately, and privacy—through the use of suitable window coverings and door(s) must be provided.

Above all, the head must have generous ventilation, some means of conserving water supplies and holding tank space, and the essential plumbing fixtures in a size and layout that can be used by real people. Many bathrooms look great in the showroom but don't have enough clearance to close the door if someone is sitting on the toilet. And even though there is usually a pullout shower head, giving the illusion that this is a proper bathroom, it's often impossible to undress, shower, and dress again in the space allowed.

Obviously, the place to start planning the head is before you buy the boat in the first place. Spend some time inside the head with the door closed, and go through the motions of showering or sitting on the toilet to see if such basic steps are physically possible.

I'm always amused at the way decorators arrange towels on show boats. They pile great, arty arrangements of pretty towels on the one dinky towel rack that the boat builder has provided. Picture the situation at the end of the day. Probably at least two people will have showered in this head at least once, and used it for the usual other ablutions, leaving it with a minimum of two damp bath towels, two wet washcloths, and a couple of limp hand towels. Add to this the pile of soiled laundry that has accumulated by the end of each day, and you have a recipe for mess, mildew, and odors quite unlike what you envisioned back in the showroom.

Some Special Tips to Consider

- A bigger, better exhaust fan to rid the head rapidly of steam and odors. A solar-powered vent fan is available from Kel/Tech Engineering Inc., 39 Varda Landing Rd., Sausalito, CA 94965.
- More, more, more towel racks. It may not be possible to get matching racks later. Add matching hooks for hanging up clothes while showering.
- Better behind-the-scenes venting. Often, serious odor problems result when the holding tank is not adequately vented to the outdoors.

Both fixed and folding brass hooks can be used in the head, lockers, and cabins.
JAMES BLISS COMPANY

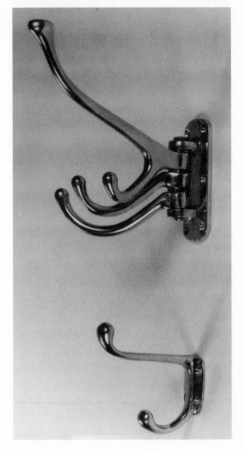

- Teak grates for the head floor to provide drier, surer footing. If the shower is a sit-down design, a teak grating on the seat will improve drainage.
- Window coverings that provide privacy day and night in crowded marinas.
- If water must be conserved, consider an at-source water heater so water is not wasted while one waits for hot water to arrive through long pipes.
- An off-on switch in the shower head will help conserve water.
- If the clothes hamper is located in the head, add as many vents to it as possible.

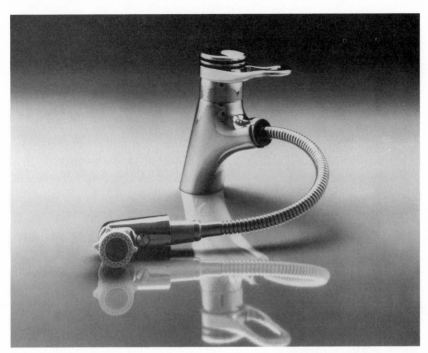

Advanced styling and marine features are trademarks of the Grohe line of faucets with pullout sprayers. In fixed position, unit serves as a faucet at the sink. Extended and placed in a holder, it becomes a shower head. GROHE AMERICA INC.

Features once found only in luxury bathrooms are now used in the most modern and upscale yacht heads. This digital faucet tells time and the water temperature. It's solar powered by whatever natural or artificial light is available in the head. U.S. BRASS

- Don't go overboard on colored fixtures because, once the head is furnished, the predominate look may be that of the towels. In the head, more than in any other area of the boat, a complete new look can be achieved with linens. With a platinum background, for example, dress the head in red towels, lid cover, bathmat, and shower curtain one season, jade green the next. An all-white bathroom can be warmed with pastels, stylized in a deep tone, or starkly sharpened with all-black accessories.
- Gold-plated fixtures used to be synonymous with conspicuous consumption. Actually, they're very practical because they don't tarnish as brass does.
- Plated plastic fixtures are in widespread use. They're inexpensive and are much lighter than solid brass.
- If the head has its own sump, use cleaners or algaecides to keep it odorfree.
- Make a discreet sign explaining to your guests how to operate fixtures.
- If you're doing major remodeling and have ample space, plan early in the project to add built-ins such as a heat lamp, wall-mount hair dryer, lighted makeup mirror, telephone, whirlpool, a scale, extra hooks or handholds, tanning light, or a sound system and/or speakers from the boat's central stereo system. Popular additions to larger heads include a compact washer-dryer, bidet, or personal workout equipment.
- If the compartment is a very small one, with no room for anything but a toilet, provide a little box where waterless hand wipes can be kept and another box where discarded towelettes and wrappers can be placed.
- Plumb in a shower on deck for after-swim rinses, to minimize the number of showers that will be taken below. Ready-made units, complete with telephone shower and stowage cabinet, are sold by marine plumbing suppliers. Simpler still, tap into a nearby cold-water line and install a sink sprayer near the swim ladder.
- Add extra sink/mirror/shaver plug/vanity areas where

possible in cabins and companionways to cut down on the amount of time each person spends in the bathroom.

Here are some offbeat ways to make a tiny bathroom seem larger or more livable:

- Raise the roof. Adding a hatch over the head will provide a few extra inches of headroom. If the head has its own hatch, have a canvas enclosure custom-made which can be placed over the open hatch while in port, much like the canvas extension used in a pop-top camper. More overhead room will be provided below without any loss of privacy.
- Lower the floor. There may be space to lower the deck

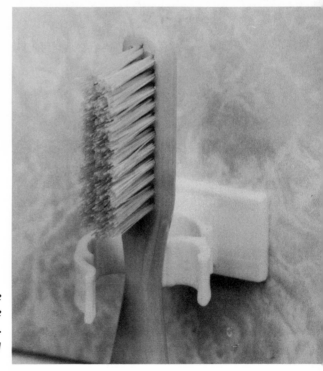

Inexpensive, self-adhesive hooks in many sizes are sold in discount stores. They hold items securely in any seas.

Lavish use of mirrors expands this small head. Mirror-faced cabinets are available in many sizes and styles.
GORDON GROENE

a few inches to provide more standing headroom. If the entire head floor can't be lowered, perhaps an area could be lowered in front of the sink or in the shower pan.

- Many head doors must be left closed at all times because they have no other stowed position. It may be possible to redesign the door so that it folds, slides, or otherwise stows in an open position. It can then be closed when privacy is desired, but left open for a more airy, spacious feeling when someone is simply making up, or doing hand laundry.
- Mirrors make a small area seem more spacious.
- It may be possible to create the illusion of more space by doing one wall in a mural wallpaper, or by having an artist do a trompe l'oeil painting on any available wall.
- Take a cue from Pullman compartments by using a sink that folds or slides back against a wall when not in use.
- Replace a solid shower door with a curtain which will allow for more air flow.
- Explore thoroughly the marine-fixtures marketplace. Marine toilets come in many sizes and profiles, some of them much more compact than others. When it comes to sinks, of course, the larger the better.
- Eliminate a door. A popular layout on many boats, both power and sail, is a head with two doors—one opening from a stateroom and the other from a passageway. Although it's nice to be able to get into the head from your cabin, the extra door means a loss of "wall" space inside the head, and a loss of space inside or outside the head wherever swinging room is provided for the doors. Replace one door, most likely the one on the cabin side, either with a solid wall or with a full-length cupboard of whatever depth can be managed with the space available. Even if it is only three or four inches deep, you have gained many cubic feet of stowage space for the head or cabin or both.
- Eliminate storage areas. If the head is one of those claustrophobia specials in which every inch is filled with cabinets, consider adding more "air" space by substituting,

67

Marine heads now come in many colors, shapes, sizes, and styles.
SEALAND TECHNOLOGY

say, a pedestal sink for a sink cabinet and plain mirrors for bulky, mirrored medicine cabinets. This will then require that the crew revert to the old boarding house practice of keeping their toiletries in their cabins, bringing their toilet kits each time they come to shower or shave. The head will not only look more spacious, it will stay neater.

- Consider rerouting plumbing. I've seen some factory plumbing jobs that were done the quickest, easiest way, taking up far too much storage room under cabinets with great pretzels of piping. Any good home improvement store now carries do-it-yourself plumbing accessories that allow the amateur to plumb with copper, as well as with the new plastics, without soldering.
- Reposition wall-mounted accessories that stick out into the room and make it look smaller. They're a menace, especially underway. One of the most painful bruises I ever received on a boat was in a shower stall where I was thrown against a sharp, wall-mounted soap dish. A

recessed toilet-tissue holder can be mounted in the side of a cabinet. You may be able to mold or carve recessed soap holders into the sink and shower. Towel rings can be substituted for some bar-type racks. Clothing hooks that fold flat when not in use are available.

Whirlpool Baths and Spas

Spas are one of the most popular of luxury additions to today's yachts, both power and sail. I've seen small spas on deck, and down below in master suites. Once a California craze, spas are so common everywhere that many yachtsmen don't want to give up their Jacuzzis when they go to sea.

A spa is a superb relaxer for tired muscles, an excellent selling point for resale or charter, a great social center when you have guests aboard. You can have one small enough to fit in a single bathtub for your private use, or a spa large enough for six or eight.

Let's talk definitions. A whirlpool is a bathtub that contains hydromassage. It is emptied after use. A spa is larger, seats two or more, and has a filter and chemicals, like a swimming pool. Water is changed only as necessary.

What's Available in Spas

The choice ranges from simple, basic spas to the most advanced, futuristic spas which have tanning lights, TV with cable and VCR, automatic beverage dispenser, hands-free video phone, digital audio sound, and computerized controls that remember each bather's individual preferences for time and temperature.

Retail prices range from about eight hundred to fifteen hundred dollars for a whirlpool bath, and two thousand dollars and up for spas, not counting installation. Shipping weights for complete spas are in the range of five hundred to one thousand pounds so, depending on water capacity, a spa can be a very

Spas and whirlpools are becoming as common on yachts as they are in homes. JACUZZI

heavy addition to your boat. Take weight, support, space, and water supply into consideration.

Although rustic wood hot tubs are popular in some areas, yachtsmen will find sleek, new acrylics more practical. White still prevails, but color is everywhere, and fixtures are softly sculpted. There is a design for everyone, from the young career couple who like to relax in the spa with friends, to the elderly arthritic who enjoys a nightly bubble bath.

From the yachtsman's standpoint, the simplest units are whirlpool baths because many of them fit a standard tub space, utilize existing hot water, and require only 110V wiring. Most are bathtubs, seating one, but some accommodate two. Installing one in a master head would be much the same as installing a conventional bathtub.

Spas are larger and heavier, seating as many as six or eight. So-called "portable" spas are self-contained, so completely that they can be used with a deck hose and a wall plug, and gravity drained. Such a spa used on deck would have to be well secured underway, but it's also easily emptied and offloaded or stowed for passage-making.

Most built-in spas come preplumbed and preassembled. You arrange for incoming water, drainage, wiring which may involve up to two 230-volt 20-amp dedicated circuits, and final hook-up, which may include remote heaters and pumps, built-in or add-on timer to control heat or filter functions over a set period (usually a week), and whatever tiling and carpentering are needed to complete the installation. You may also need additional discharge pump capacity, depending on the amount of water and length of lift.

Advertising brochures accent style and features rather than remodeler convenience, and none of the literature deals with the special requirements for yacht use, so you'll have to do some research. It won't be hard to find a size and shape to fit almost any space you have available for a spa. Choose from square, rectangular, free-form, octagonal, or corner models for platform or sunken installation.

Although most spas are acrylic, perhaps reinforced with fiberglass, the type and quality of insulation differs. Comparison shop, because a proper under-pan will minimize leakage, mildew, and the danger of rot. Some brands provide a full pan underneath, and a waterproof insulation skin, to avoid such problems.

Installation must be done in concert with plumbing and electrical work, so involve a spa in your planning as early as possible. Access to equipment and controls must be provided for. If tile is involved, make sure the tile setter is familiar with spas; grouts must be able to resist harsh, pool-type chemicals.

One more tip: Make sure the manufacturer packages the unit very well for shipping, because even minor damage can cause lengthy installation delays. Ideally, the manufacturer will package so that tubs remain wrapped after uncrating and during most of the installation process.

A Whirlpool Dictionary

Air-activated switch. Some spa controls are bellows-activated, a user safety feature that eliminates a chance of a wet bather contacting a live switch.

Air blower. Some spas have a blower that releases air into the water through holes in the shell.

Dry-run protection. Protects against burnout if the pump is run without water.

Floor loading. In spas it ranges from eighty to one hundred or more pounds per square foot; in whirlpool baths, forty to fifty-five pounds per square foot.

Freeze protector. Optional sensor that turns on the pump/heater circuit when water temperature falls below a preset temperature.

Gate valves. Optional valves that isolate the tub from the support system, so tub does not have to be drained to clean the filter or work on the pump or heater.

Hiss. The flow of air that mixes with the water is handled differently by manufacturers, making some whirlpools more noisy than others.

Hot tub. Whirlpool spa in wood.

IAPMO. International Association of Plumbing and Mechanical Officials. Sets industry standards. Look for both UL and IAPMO label.

Lounger. Refers to the shape of the spa. Some have seats only; loungers permit bathers to recline.

Portable. Self-contained; does not have to be plumbed and wired in. Will need special anchoring if placed on deck, but is easily removed for passage-making.

Remote pack. Motors and pumps installed elsewhere to filter, heat, and agitate water.

Safety suction. Device that breaks suction when something blocks the return on a whirlpool system. Prevents injury when body comes in contact with suction return.

Skirt. Some units come with a skirt, others with optional skirt; some have no skirt at all, requiring you to devise skirt or platform.

Tile flange kit. Flexible material that fits between the tub rim and whatever tile provided by the installer.

Trip-Level Drain. Regular up-down lever bathtub drain.

Whirlpool bath. A bathtub that contains a built-in hydromassage system. Uses hot water from your on-board water heater, and is drained after each use.

Whirlpool spa. A unit that includes pump, motor, heater, filter, and jet hydromassage. It is kept filled for days at a time before cleaning, and needs chemical treatment.

FABRICS AND WINDOW TREATMENTS

Plain or plaid, man-made or natural, billowy or burlap, fabrics are the warming touch atop the woods, metals, and plastics that are the bones of your boat. Textiles, like so many other materials used in the boating life, have improved immensely in recent years.

On the practical side are new coatings for both indoor and outdoor fabrics, making them less susceptible to stains, mildew, leakage, flammability, and breakdown caused by the damaging ultraviolet spectrum of the sun's rays.

From the esthetics standpoint there are many new designer fabrics and matching wallpapers. Although they're sold through home centers, most of them have features such as stainproofers and strippability that are important in yacht installations. On your boat as well as at home, you want fabrics that shrug off stains, and wall coverings that clean easily and, when the time comes, strip off in one piece without hours of steaming, digging, and scraping.

You no longer have to limit your fabric shopping to marine stores and awning makers. Every big upholstery shop and fabric store carries fabrics that can, nautically speaking, stand the gaff.

In fact, the crossover market has become so strong that one decorator showed me two fabrics that appeared to be identical. She'd paid twenty-five dollars a yard at a marine source for the same acrylic-coated cotton that she bought from an upholstery supply house for four fifty a yard. And, she assured me, both the coating and the fabric had all the features needed to meet her own, rigid standards.

This isn't to say that she would buy household leather to upholster a sofa for a sunny saloon, or just any canvas to use for deck cushions. It tells me, though, that with persistent shopping all of us can now get durable fabrics that will stand up in the marine environment even though we live in areas where there are no marine fabric stores.

Don't overlook the home-improvement marketplace as a possible source of wallcoverings for the boat. Matching and coordinating fabrics are often available with Teflon soil-and-stain repellent.
RAINTREE DESIGNS

When shopping for any fabrics to be used in decorating your boat, here are elements to consider. Your supplier should be able to answer most, and perhaps all, of your questions regarding the following:

Backing. How many plies are in this fabric? Is the backing itself guaranteed not to break down or bleed through? A common problem only a few years ago was that the backings of some marine vinyls bled through as an indelible pink stain. Backings on other fabrics delaminate, become brittle, or otherwise break down and damage a finished product. Ask not only about the face fabric, but the makeup of the entire material.

Cleanability code. It will be listed in specifications when you're shopping for a fabric. If you're looking at bolts of fabric, the code may be stamped on the selvage edge or printed on bolt or wrapper. In a finished piece, it will probably appear somewhere on a label. W means the fabric can be cleaned with water, S stands for solvent, S/W means the fabric can be cleaned with either solvent or water. X means vacuum only.

Colorfastness. Of all the specifications I've tried to wring out of suppliers, colorfastness is the one they were most coy about. Some fabric manufacturers have done extensive testing, and advertise their fabrics' colorfastness proudly. Others either don't know, or don't want you to know, how well a fabric or a particular dye will stand up to repeated washings, sunnings, or abrasion. Among similar fabrics, some dyes may be more stable than others.

Finish. Has the fabric been stainproofed? With what? Before or after fabrication of the finished piece? Keep in mind that such coatings don't increase the durability of fabrics. That is determined by the fiber, how it was woven, and how it's used. Most fabrics should be retreated regularly. Ask your decorator to get manufacturer instructions for cleaning and care.

Flame retardant. Some fabrics have been specially treated and will not support combustion. Most others can be treated with a spray-on flame retardant. A combination flame retardant–water repellent spray is also available. So is a silicone water repellent which is not itself a flameproofer but which can be used without affecting existing flame-resistant properties in treated fabrics.

Where technical specs for fabrics are available, several references may be given, indicating flame spread and smoke development.

Light reflectance. Peter Granata, president of Granata Design in Hilton Head, creates interiors for racy, upscale Cobalt cruisers. "Sometimes mirrors are overdone," he says, "but a dull area can also be brightened with a metallic or bright-finish fabric." You might want to consider using chintz or pearlized vinyl instead of mirrors in areas that need more brightness.

Linings. In many instances, lining a bedspread, curtain, or an upholstery fabric can increase its sound-absorbing qualities, make it hang or lie better, and make it stronger. The wrong lining, however, can shrink at different rates from the fabric, act as a host for mildew, or bleed through if wet.

Ounces per yard. Weight is an important consideration in indoor-outdoor textiles such as canvas and duck. Weights of ten to eighteen or twenty ounces are usually specified. The lighter the fabric, the more supple and malleable. Heavier weights (in fabrics that are otherwise the same) mean increased strength and water resistance.

Seam slippage. This is one of the technical specs that your decorator will want to take into consideration.

Tear rate. Where toughness is important, you may be able to get manufacturer specs on a fabric's tear rate. The stronger the tear resistance, the less likely the problem of further damage if, say, a vinyl seat is accidentally slashed by a gaff. Tensile strength may also be available. Be sure to request mending instructions, and any needed supplies, from the manufacturer.

UV resistance. Some manufacturers are coy about releasing independent lab reports about the effectiveness of their ultraviolet treatments. Try to get complete specs if possible. Buy from a reliable supplier who has a wide choice of outdoor, marine, and awning fabrics, rather than just one line, and let him recommend one that is best for your use.

Resilience and wrinkling. The fabric on upholstered pieces should be able to spring back to shape in concert with the foam underneath.

Shrink rate. Some fabrics, especially in the canvas and duck line, are preshrunk. In those that are not, a shrink rate of 2 percent or so must be part of your planning. This should be clearly stated in specs. Many other fabrics, especially the new synthetics, are inherently shrinkproof.

Print. Generally, a monochrome look is best because it makes small spaces feel larger. Different patches of color cut up a room, making it appear smaller. A bold print can be used for a dramatic look on a big bedspread, headboard, or an accent chair, but smaller prints, weaves, plaids, and textures are best—not just because they appear larger but because they mask minor smudges and spills better than solid colors do.

Warranty. Read the fine print. You may have to fill out and file a form at the time of purchase. If any warranty applies, it probably means only that new fabric, not the cost of labor, will be supplied to replace the material that failed.

Water permeability. Manufacturer specs should be available. Compare them when shopping for fabrics to be used in applications where water resistance is important.

Wear. Wear rate is expressed in different ways on spec sheets. One of the most common is the Wyzenbeek/wire screen test (ASTM D-1175). Wear rates are reported in "rubs."

Vinyls

No longer cheap substitutes, today's lush and lustrous two- and three-ply vinyls have a place in any decorating scheme. Work with an upholsterer who knows these materials. Some vinyls have a better "memory" than others (i.e. they recover faster after a cushion has been sat on), some have better seam strength, or are better for the sharper tailoring required in tight corners. It depends on usage, and whether you want the fit to be loose and lively, such as in seat cushions, or extremely taut and tight, as in a headboard or banquette. In any case, the fabricator should use the right needle, right stitches per inch, and the right thread for the material.

One of the industry's new buzz words is "interference pigments" which are platelets coated with a thin film of a plastic with

Leatherlike vinyls are lush, lustrous, scrubbable, and tough-wearing. Hundreds of colors and textures are available. AQUALINE

a higher refractive index than the base fabric. The look is a deep, rich, pearlized sheen which is smashing in the appropriate setting.

Vinyls are available in dozens of textures, from glassy smooth to diamond or dot patterns to deep leather grains, and in so many colors that it's possible to match almost any shade in your decorating palette. Sheens range from matte to the pearlescents mentioned above.

PreFixx is a new coating from Nautolex that, in laboratory tests, withstood 60–75,000 test cycles compared with 6,000 for untreated Nautolex. Very difficult stains such as ballpoint ink can be cleaned with solvents which would damage ordinary vinyls. Complete cleaning instructions come with any PreFixx treated fabric.

Clear vinyls for use as windows in cockpit enclosures or dodgers are sold in various gauges, usually from .012 to .040. Discuss with your fabricator which thickness would be best for your application. Flame-retardant transparent flexible vinyls are available.

Suede

New man-made suedes are amazing, but here, more than in almost any other fabric, it's important to compare technical specs. Some imitation suedes are nothing more than cheap synthetics that will pill and wear very quickly. Others, such as Novasuede and Ultrasuede HP, have superior looks, feel, heft, and workability and are almost indestructible, at a third the weight of genuine leather suede of the same tensile strength.

Minor spots and burns can be removed with fine sandpaper. Water-based stains can be cleaned with mild soap and water; solvents can be used on others. Light stains and smudges can be lifted off with the sticky side of cellophane tape. It's no wonder suede is taking off as the look of the decade!

If you prefer a real leather suede, get one that was fabricated for marine or automotive use rather than a household quality. It will stand up better to temperature extremes, sun damage, and other abuses. If you don't have a marine fabric specialist in your area, talk to an automotive upholstery shop.

Specialty Marine Fabrics

Here's a partial list of specialty marine fabrics that fulfill special uses on deck or in wet or heavy use below. I found that many decorators didn't know the generic term for their favorite fabrics, which could mean that you are sold high-priced Frustle instead of lower-priced and equally good Frumble simply because your decorator doesn't know that fristlized cotton is available under many different brand names. Where possible, try to determine what generic material is best for the project, then get specifications on more than one brand, and compare.

I'm indebted to Donald J. Miller, general manager at Reliatex Inc., 6004 Bonacker Dr., Tampa, FL 33610, who has always been quick and able in answering my questions about marine fabrics. Reliatex is a wholesaler to southeastern markets and does not sell to the public, but I highly recommend that your marine decorator, upholsterer, or canvas maker contact Miller for information about any marine materials, threads, fasteners, and foams. For the trade only, the telephone is (800)282-9121, or (813)621-6021.

Acrylics. Available both in woven fabrics and as a coating, this miracle man-made material can be found in many vibrant colors. Acrylics are fairly inert, Miller says, and have excellent resistance to ultraviolet damage. In all its forms, weaves and qualities—e.g., acrylic-coated polyester or acrylic-coated woven acrylic—it is water resistant, which means that, while it's not completely watertight, it breathes. It's a popular choice for boat covers and seat covers.

Clear vinyl. Used as windows in cockpit enclosures, clear vinyl is available in various gauges (thicknesses). Your fabricator should shoot for a good compromise—thick enough for hard wear, but thin and supple enough for clear viewing and for easy folding and stowing.

Duck. This refers to a weave. It's a coarse, hard-wearing fabric available in cotton, acrylic, polyester, and blends.

Expanded-vinyl upholstery fabrics. Two types of vinyl fabrics are in general use: Expanded vinyl has been fused to a knit backing and is best for seat constructions where sharp, highly tailored details are desired; vinyls with nonwoven backing, called fuzzyback vinyls in the industry, are the same thickness but have a softer drape. They're better for tufts and other softer detailing. Both types are available from many manufacturers.

Fiberglass screening. One type, which both screens and darkens, is Thermoscreen, a PVC-coated fiberglass screening sold by 3G Mermet Corporation, 3965 Virginia Ave., Cincinnati, OH 45227.

Fire-resistant duck. It's always a plus on a boat to order fire-resistant fabrics. Most marine coatings are not, in themselves, fire resistant but special treatments can be added.

Mineral-dyed duck. Anyone who was boating twenty years ago probably had mineral-dyed cotton duck, perhaps treated with something to make it more water resistant, aboard in spray shields, dodgers, and cushion covers in the classic pearl gray color. It's being outsold now by the newer acrylics but it's breathable, cheaper than the newer fabrics, and is still a popular choice with many fabricators.

Thermoscreen is made from PVC-coated fiberglass. It can be installed as screens, or made into roller, guided, or vertical blinds. It eliminates 80–90 percent of solar heat, and during cold weather reduces heat loss to the outside by up to 25 percent. THERMOSCREEN

Sailcloth. It's available in dozens of weights, colors, and fibers. Because they are strong and usually UV resistant, heavy sail-cloths are a good choice for stuff bags, lighter weights for curtains.

Three-ply waterproof vinyl laminates. Sold under such names as Herculite, Weblon, and Aquatex II, these consist of two layers of waterproof fabric which are laminated, sandwich-style, with scrim in the middle for strength. Such laminates are usually used for bimini tops and waterproof cockpit enclosures.

Vinyl-coated boat-top fabric. A time-honored coating, vinyl is also available in a laminated version which is less expensive than the coated type. Usually used on cottons, the vinyl is absorbed by the fabric and thus achieves an excellent bond.

Vinyl-encapsulated woven polyester. This is the general term for the new, water-shedding weaves that are used on outdoor furniture. They dry almost immediately, and are a good choice for upholstered cockpit furniture.

Vivatex. Long a popular brand name that many boat owners use as a fabric name, this is a coating that is available in more than one fabric. It's usually used to coat cottons or blends.

Cleaning Seats, Upholstery and Marine Vinyl Flooring

The first consideration is to keep vinyl-covered cushions away from the wet. When it rains, stow them below or seams will trap and absorb water. Off-season, stow cushions in a dry, well-ventilated spot. Wash all vinyls at least once a week with a soft cloth, mild laundry detergent, and warm water, and towel dry.

For ballpoint ink stains, clean immediately with rubbing alcohol and rinse with warm water. For insect repellents and suntan lotions, wipe clean immediately and wash area with mild laundry detergent and warm water. Rinse with cloths repeatedly wrung out in clean water. Avoid saturating upholstered pieces. Flooring or slipcovers can be cleaned with a rinse, but dry them immediately and thoroughly.

Sport Topping

Referring to a polyester-cotton-blend fabric which it makes for use in cockpit enclosures, dodgers, and other deck accessories, Aqualine Marine Vinyls suggests the following cleaning procedures. Unless the manufacturer of your topping suggests otherwise, these guidelines should work for any similar fabrics. Clean with warm water and a mild laundry detergent; wipe dry with a clean cloth. For stubborn stains or mildew, use a stiff bristle brush. To prevent mildew, Aqualine advises, never store a wet top folded or rolled.

Aqualine recommends against using solvents, carbon tet, janitorial cleaners, scouring agents, undiluted bleach, or gasoline on vinyls. Powdered abrasives, steel wool, and industrial-strength cleaners will dull surfaces and are not recommended. Dry-cleaning fluids and lacquer solvents are especially harmful because they attack vinyl, remove pattern and color, or otherwise disturb the surface. A test patch in an inconspicuous area is always a good idea.

Surf Craft Fabrics makes the following recommendations for cleaning its high quality, Scotchgard-protected, acrylic fabrics: To remove stains, soak for twenty minutes in a solution of four ounces Clorox and four ounces Ivory Flakes in one gallon of lukewarm water. (Although rinsing isn't indicated, I assume that a thorough rinse should follow.) To machine wash, use cold cycle and, in each load, sixteen ounces Clorox and eight ounces Ivory Flakes. Always line dry. Don't use hot water, hot drying, or a hot iron or steam press.

A Caveat About Cleaning

While the suggestions above may be right for the fabrics indicated, you can see that they vary. It's always best to get cleaning instructions from the manufacturer of each fabric used in your boat. They are available to your fabricator or decorator; insist on getting them at the time the fabric is ordered or the finished work delivered. File them, and review them as needed. It could be difficult to track them down later.

To use bleach where it is verboten, or to put a fabric in a dryer when it should be line-dried, could not only compromise the piece's looks and wearability but would void the guarantee.

Indoor-Outdoor Fabrics

Coated fabrics have come into the space age, offering the supple workability and breathability of a canvaslike weave, plus the col-

orfastness and water resistance of vinyl. Although such fabrics
are used primarily on deck for sunshades, dodgers, and upholstery, they are a practical and tough fabric for use down below
in spots that get a lot of hard wear. Consider coated canvas for
bedspreads in children's cabins, for sofas where people sit while
wearing wet, salty bathing suits or foul-weather gear, and for
protective, temporary covers almost anywhere below.

These fabrics are also good for making laundry and stuff bags,
PFD storage bags, and garment bags.

Fabric tips

- If you're not sure whether a fabric will "pill," rub a sample repeatedly with a pencil eraser.
- To check whether a fabric will wrinkle easily, crush a
  handful and release it.
- Flammability is tested in obvious ways. Because cigarette burns are the most common damage on upholstery,
  see what happens when you hold a lit cigarette to a
  swatch of the fabric.
- Keep notes on all fabric cleaning/care instructions.
  Sometimes they appear on the selvage edge, sometimes
  on a label on the end of the bolt. On a finished product,
  a care label is probably sewn in. Your decorator should
  be able to supply complete cleaning instructions from
  each fabric manufacturer. Request them as each fabric
  is ordered; it may be difficult to track them down later.
- The tighter the weave, the stronger the fabric and the
  less likely it is to pull and snag. A tightly woven linen or
  silk can be stronger than a loosely woven synthetic.
- Bud Pettisani of Aqua Marine Products suggests quilting
  or outline stitching as a way to add interest to a plain
  fabric.

Fabric manufacturers include:

American Recreational Products
500 Orchard St.,
New Haven, MO 63068

Astrup Corp.
2937 W. 25th St.
Cleveland, OH 44113

B&B Interiors
54835 C.R. 19
Bristol, IN 46507

John Boyle and Co.
P.O. Box 791
Statesville, NC 28677

Bruin Plastics
P.O. Box 175 Main St.
Clendale, RI 02826

Burch Mfg.
618 First Ave. N.
Ft. Dodge, IA 50501

Carrousel
1940 S. West Blvd.
Vineland, NJ 08360

Coated Fabrics Division
Gencoro
3729 Twining St.
Toledo, OH 43696

C. R. Daniels
3451 Ellicott Center Dr.
Ellicott City, MD 21043

Douglass Industries
412 Boston Ave.
Egg Harbor, NJ 08215

Glen Raven Mills Inc.
1831 North Park Ave.
Glen Raven, NC 27215

Haartz Corp
P.O. Box 286
Acton, MA 01720

Herculite Products
Health-Chem
1107 Broadway
New York, NY 10010

Isratech Marketing
200 Madison Ave.
New York, NY 10016

Jessup Mfrg.
P.O. Box 366
McHenry, IL 60050

J. P. Stevens Co.
33 Stevens St.
Greenville, SC 29602

Soundcoat
1 Burt Dr.
Deerpark, NY 11729

Uniroyal Fabrics
312 N. Hill St.
Mishawaka, IN 46544

U.S. Laminating
100 Wilbur Pl.
Bohemia, NY 11716

Weblon
P.O. Box 190
Port Chester, NY 10573

West Point Pepperell
P.O. Box 71
West Point, GA 31833

Window Treatments

Nautically speaking, a window is a transparent place in a sail, but once again, I'll depart from approved marine terminology and apply the term *window* to any porthole, port light, windshield, or hatch that must be dealt with as a window.

Window coverings are important in keeping heat and harsh sun out of the boat. In marinas where you're no more than a few feet from the nearest neighbor, curtains are essential for privacy. Too, the right window treatments can absorb noise; the wrong ones propagate or create it.

Although curtains are a familiar and favorite topic with most decorators, none of the rules on land apply to a boat. Many windows aren't even symmetrical, let alone a standard size, so ready-made draperies and hardware can't be used. Special hardware, in rustproof materials, must be found.

Some windows slant in such a way that curtains can't be hung from a rod at the top of the window. In most hulls, there is at least a 5–15-degree angle from the top of a rod to the bottom of a curtain left hanging free. In some windshields, the angle is more like 45 degrees. So, rods have to be provided at both top and bottom of such windows.

There are reasons for not allowing curtains to swing free. One is that they'll wear more quickly from constant abrasion. Also, watching a swaying curtain can cause seasickness in some of the staunchest stomachs aboard, so ways have to be devised to secure window coverings top and bottom, open and closed.

Aboard some boats, I've seen portholes that were six to eight inches deeper than the cabin's "walls." They present no place to mount a curtain and, when the porthole opens in, clearance must be provided. Usually, each porthole area must be boxed in and the curtain or shutter mounted on the box itself.

Wood and vinyl blinds and shutters, which are so popular in homes, are clattery underway. When you're at anchor and running the generator, nonfabric blinds reflect sound; fabrics cushion it.

Ideally, then, you're looking for window treatments that are in harmony with decor but which also let in light, keep out light, provide privacy, minimize noise, and allow the window to open or close normally. That's a tall order.

Aesthetics aside, there are countless solutions for each prob-

Pleated shades can be ordered with bottom holddown bracket. They're available in a large choice of colors in sheer and opaque fabrics. For information: Elkhart Door Inc., P.O. Box 2177, Elkhart IN 46515. ELKHART DOOR INC.

lem, depending not just on personal tastes but on priorities. If you like to sleep late in the morning, for example, you'll want the best, darkest black-out curtains. If you want to be awakened by the earliest light, you'll want the thinnest curtains consistent with your need for privacy at the dock.

In the tropics or in very cold climates, you can add layers of insulation to window coverings. Or, if merely keeping sunlight out of the boat is your goal, reflective window coatings and/or curtain linings could take precedence.

If you always anchor out, miles from anyone else, you may not care about privacy. In narrow marina berths, tightly closed blinds are a defense against everything from bash-and-grab thieves to peeping toms. Let's look at some of the possibilities:

For areas where a very thin curtain is needed, Peter Granata likes washable silks, saying "they have no bad side." He also works sometimes with sandblasting, to make a window opaque. "Experiment first with cheap glass," he advises. "Cardboard seems to make the best mask, because it gives a little. Rigid masks break down faster." Sandblaster attachments are available now to fit home air compressors.

Vicky Moses of Oceanic Designs in Daytona Beach uses marine drapery track top and bottom to assure a taut, tailored fit. "And we do our own measuring," she says. "Drapery shops never seem to get the right measurements on boats." Moses also uses dim-out fabrics to line most of her draperies. It protects the drapery fabric from sun fade, without blocking daylight from the cabin.

All professional yacht decorators have access to a large choice of drapery styles and hardware. Traditional pinch-pleat styles are still popular. So are all the curtain styles now being seen in homes: bouffants, shutters, vertical or horizontal miniblinds, valance and lambrequin treatments, and pleated and roller shades of all kinds.

Frankly, the place I look first for almost anything in the line of furnishings is the Sears catalog. Even if I don't find what I want there, I have learned a lot about what is trendy this year, what's available (at least in the household market), and what things cost. If, then, I find that vinyl or aluminum miniblinds from a marine supplier would cost four times more than Sears prices, and they still contain just as much steel as Sears's do, I question the advantage of buying them from a marine decorator.

Through the catalog, for example, you can find ready-made and custom window coverings in many styles as well as wood, plastic, and brass-plated hardware. Sears also carries a clear Lexan curtain rod, and a large selection of aluminum and enameled-steel shower rods.

Truly rustproof nylon, stainless steel, and plastic curtain hardware is available from marine sources, but the selection of styles is limited. (When in doubt, test with a magnet.) Where rustproof hardware isn't available you can make your own curtain rods, as Gordon and I did, out of brass rod and brass fittings.

However, if you're going to get hardware that will eventually rust—and you may choose to because that is the size, color, and style you want—you may as well get it at the most reasonable price available through Sears, J. C. Penney's, or your local department store.

Among clever window coverings I've seen used effectively on boats are:

- In the wheelhouse of a motor sailer, spring-loaded shades were mounted on windshield windows. A tab on the bottom of each shade slipped over a fastener to hold the shade taut when down.
- Small galley portholes were covered with linen dish towels in a suitable color and pattern. The towels were cut down to fit, then hemmed to shir over a rod.
- A tasteful macramé hanging was made to fit over a small portlight.
- A quick, easy way to attach a curtain to a fuzzy headliner surface is to sew half a hook-and-loop fastener to the curtain. It grips the fuzz almost as securely as a matching piece of hook-and-loop. It's not recommended for curtains that are opened and closed often, says Peter Granata, because the continued pulling eventually begins to lift the fabric, which has to be given a "haircut."
- Clear vinyl, when used for curtain tiebacks, lets the cur-

tain material show through. Or, have pieces of clear acrylic bent to the needed shape, and attach them to the boat to serve as curtain holdbacks.

- Many types of shutters are available, not just traditional louvered types, but shutters that have stained or frosted-glass inserts and others which use shirred fabric inserts. They come ready to paint or stain; brass or stainless-steel hinges can easily be substituted for the plated brass which is usually provided. Marine decorators especially like the fabric insert types, both to utilize a fabric that appears elsewhere in the cabin and to provide a sound-absorbing window covering.

About Fasteners

The strength and durability of any fabric aboard a yacht depends on what threads and findings are used. Rusty steel or corroded aluminum zippers, bleeding grommets, and dissolving stitches often spell early death for good fabric.

Where snap fasteners, zippers, hook-and-loop, or other extras are to be incorporated into a project, discuss the choices with at least two sources, e.g., the canvas shop and one of their customers who has had a couple of years experience with a similar product; or the fabric manufacturer and a marine upholstery expert.

You need to know how the fastener will hold up in a particular use, in a particular fabric. It could be that the canvas shop will steer you away from a particular fastener because, even though it's easier for you to use, it's hard for them to install. Or a past customer will give a bad report on a good fabric because he didn't maintain it properly. Or a supplier will tout the fabric that carries the highest markup.

By talking to two or three sources, all of them coming at the project from different directions, you'll be better able to sort out the truth.

~~~~~~

Chapter 6

HIT THE DECK: FLOOR COVERINGS

~~~~~~

Aboard your yacht, floor* covering is more than a decorator advantage. It can help dampen the vibration and roar of engines and generators, provide a nonskid surface for safer footing underway, and cushion the fall when frisky seas send people or objects tumbling.

Used on deck, all-weather carpeting fills all these roles and, in addition, provides a cool surface to bare feet. It is also less glary than gel coat in bright sun.

Choosing a Flooring

Wood Flooring

Pro: For mellow, salty good looks it's hard to beat the scrubbed, shiny glow of a teak-holly, teak-rubber, or solid oak floor. Wood is easy to sweep or wash, and it's among the most durable and repairable of all floorings.

Con: Wood can look cold and utilitarian, and its temperature

* For the purposes of this chapter, the word *floor* is used to refer to living areas, and *deck* to refer to outdoor areas of the boat.

and sound insulating properties are modest. While a layer of wood may absorb some engine noise, it echoes back ambient noise within the cabin itself when the engine is not running. Wet wood rots. When hidden areas (e.g., under a galley sink, or behind a piece of furniture) stay damp and fungal rot sets it, major damage results.

Wood is more expensive than carpeting and, while it needs less day-by-day care, the piper must be paid eventually. Refinishing is a major project and replacement is very costly.

New plywoods, which combine a veneer of teak or oak over a backing of less costly woods, look like the real thing. They're very durable but, once serious wear begins, cannot be sanded down year after year for refinishing.

Special Tips: Add a touch of luxury, softness, and noise reduction to an existing wood floor with a fine oriental or custom-weave area rug. An area rug can be rolled up and stowed in dirty weather, and is easily off-loaded for professional dry cleaning.

Rubbery nonskid mats which can be placed under throw rugs are found in carpeting stores and in specialty catalogs. One manufacturer is Vantage Industries, P.O. Box 43944, Atlanta, GA 30336, telephone (404)691-9500. The company's Scoot-Gard is available in 22" X 44" and 36" X 57" carpet pads and in foot-wide rolls up to one hundred feet.

Rugs can also be secured with the Velcro hold-down system or with two-sided carpet tapes which are sold in hardware and discount stores. Unlike the nonskid mats, which are easily removed and stowed, both these choices involve sticking something to the floor itself. The only advantage to stick-down installations, compared to nonskid mats, is that an area rug is secured more tightly and is easier to vacuum.

A new wrinkle on the classic inlaid teak deck has been developed by a company called GMT. Their decking system is made to order, to fit your existing deck or floor. It's solid teak, which GMT glues together and then caulks, planes, and trims to order. You have to measure carefully and send a template of your deck with the order. The new teak deck can be installed by anyone with moderate skills who follows the instructions provided.

It can be put over wood, fiberglass, steel, or aluminum. Two-part glue is provided; the floor is then caulked with a flexible silicone sealant. Prices start at twenty dollars per square foot. For information write to GMT Inc., 6116 21st St., E., Bradenton, FL 34203.

Carpeting

Pro: The decorator choices are endless. It is hard to argue against the posh, plush look and feel of thick and luxurious carpeting which is available color coordinated in the many styles, shades, and patterns of today's marketplace.

New fibers and stainproofers make carpeting a more practical choice than it once was. Carpeting absorbs sound, feels good underfoot, covers imperfections and irregularities, and anchors furniture so well that, aboard most houseboats and other fair-weather yachts, no further hold-downs are needed. Too, carpeting can be a very inexpensive choice.

Con: Carpeting holds moisture, is cumbersome to clean, and will be subject to at least some sun fading, staining, traffic patterning, or other ills. Carpeting is not recommended for the galley or head.

Special tip: New household carpetings are dazzling, tough, and stain resistant, which makes them a realistic choice for any yacht from the most luxurious to the hardest-working sportfisherman, but don't rule out the possibility of using marine carpeting down below until you've seen the rich, new olefins. They're thick and lush, not at all like the thin, cheap-looking olefin carpetings of a decade ago.

Indoor-Outdoor Carpeting

Pro: New olefin and solution-dyed polyester carpetings sold for use on deck are tough, fadeproof, and won't mildew. They provide sound deadening, skidproofing, and glare reduction, and come in a big choice of decorator colors. New chemistry makes them brighter, more durable, and less subject to breakdown from ultraviolet damage. Dye pigments are added to the molten polymer solution, so there is no fading as the carpet wears.

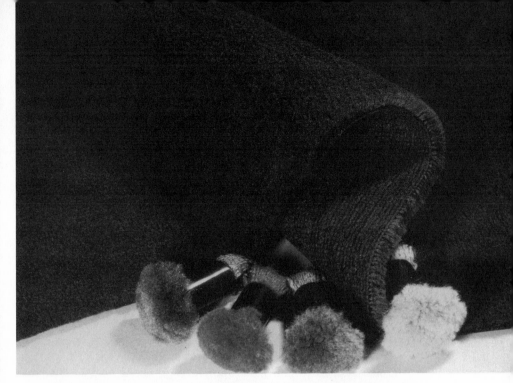

Alpha olefin fiber shows superior crush resistance and tough wear. It can be used outdoors, yet is thick and luxurious enough for use down below. The fiber is used by many leading marine carpet manufacturers.
PHILLIPS FIBERS

Easily cleaned, these carpetings can be scrubbed with suds, then hosed off. They drain quickly, and air dry in an hour or so. They are also almost indestructible. A side benefit is that some companies, such as Foss Manufacturing (231 Neck Rd., Haverhill, MA 01830) make entire lines of nonwoven fabrics in the same colors in many different thicknesses, so it's possible to get an exact match in, say, floor covering and hull liner.

A new olefin, Alpha by Phillips Fibers, proved to be even more resilient than traditional olefins. Measuring recovery after sixty seconds, a laboratory found that Alpha bounced back from a deeply compressed state twice as well as standard olefin. An hour after being compressed, the standard olefin had recovered 90 percent and the Alpha almost 350 percent.

Alpha, which is being used by a number of marine carpet manufacturers, is said to be more abrasion resistant than polyester, and more color stable, ultraviolet stable, stain resistant, and cleanable than polyester or nylon.

Con: Outdoor carpeting sheds water but, compared to paint or teak on deck, it can host enough dampness to develop a musty look and smell. Moisture problems can be avoided with good surface preparation, and proper bedding of screws in hold-down strips and other fittings, before and during installation. Otherwise, water can be trapped unseen under carpeting and can cause wood rot.

Prestige lines of indoor-outdoor carpetings are varied, deep piled, and as plush as any indoor carpeting, but some indoor-outdoor carpetings, especially the metallics, can look glitzy and cheap. When choosing a carpeting, make sure that the backing and binding are also made with colorfast, rotproof, mildewproof, ultraviolet-resistant materials.

A synthetic carpet cushion recommended by Vicky Moses of Oceanic Designs is Hartex. "Sponge-type carpet padding is just that—sponge," says Moses. "It holds water and soon it and the entire boat have a sour, mildew smell. Hartex won't hold moisture, and it has a Class A [highest in its category] flame rating," she says.

Other Choices

The obvious choices for both floors and decks are carpeting or wood. Here are some other ways you might cover or refresh your boat.

Refinish gel coat floors. If your boat has fiberglass floors with a built-in nonskid grid that has become dull and unattractive, consider refinishing with two-part polyurethane paints such as Awlgrip or Imron.

Brush-on, two-part epoxy paints are available for do-it-yourself application, and many amateurs get dazzling results. However, these paints do require a knack, and they are picky about temperatures, timing, and other application factors, so spray-on application by a professional is safest if you want a perfect result. (Do-it-yourselfers should not try spraying these paints; they require special know-how, equipment, and safeguards.)

No-wax vinyl flooring is bright, easy care, and inexpensive. It can be a plus in the galley and head, but shouldn't be used in places that get excessive sun or water. It can delaminate.

Antifatigue matting. Through restaurant and industrial sources, and sometimes through swimming pool suppliers, you can find thick, resilient, perforated rubber flooring that is about three-eighths-inch thick. Spills, crumbs, and debris fall through the gridwork to the floor. Although you'll still have to deal with the mess eventually, you aren't wading around in it during meal preparation.

These mattings are highly resilient, so most plates and glasses, when dropped, merely bounce and do not break. It's the most skidproof of floorings, even when wet or greasy, and it will cut the noise level in the galley dramatically.

At cleaning time, roll up the matting and take it on deck for a thorough sudsing and rinse. The galley floor is now bared for a thorough scrub.

Teak grating works much the same way, providing a dry, clean, raised platform over the galley or head floor. Grating is available in several thicknesses (ranging from quarter-inch to half-inch) through marine catalogs such as *Boat/US*.

Teak is extremely tolerant of wetness and harsh sun, but for good looks and long life it should be oiled regularly. Used in the shower, teak accumulates soap scum and water deposits which should be scrubbed away weekly.

Fortunately, almost every manufacturer of boat cleaners offers at least one teak-care product and most offer a large choice of teak-care systems. Try them all until you find the one best suited for the purpose. The cleaner/oil you use in the head will probably be different from the one that you find best for use in the harsh sunlight on deck.

Because teak requires regular care, it's a good idea to order grating in manageable pieces that can be removed easily to the deck or dock where they can be scrubbed and hosed.

Unglazed tile makes a lustrous, lifetime floor covering for the galley or head, but applying it is not a job for amateurs. Get advice from a full-service tile dealer who can provide one of the new, highly skid-resistant tiles with the right backings, beddings, and grouts to go with it. Make sure he knows you're installing the tile on a boat, with its twisting loads, high humidity, wettings, and mildew problems, because a great many specialty grout and mortar formulations are now available. (See p. 124.)

The drawbacks to tile include its comparatively heavy weight and its hardness. Anything dropped on it is likely to shatter. For flooring use, of course, you should choose one of the tiles that can get wet without becoming slippery.

Polyurethane Anti-Skid. Manufactured by Viscom International, Inc., 244 Farms Village Rd., West Simsbury, CT 06093, TBS Anti-Skid Surface is 100 percent polyurethane. Although it is an effective skidproofer, it doesn't have the gritty feel of surfaces treated with sand or nutshells. It's scrubbable, supple enough to install easily over nonflat surfaces, and is resistant to ultraviolet, oil, and grease.

Although it's sold primarily for use on deck, it can also be used effectively in the galley, head, or companionways. It cuts easily with scissors and can be put down permanently with epoxy or polyurethane adhesives, or installed temporarily with two-sided tape. Best of all, it comes in ten colors. Lonplate, another resilient vinyl sheet flooring with a nonskid grid molded in, is available from Lonseal, Inc., 928 E. 238th St., Bldg. A., Carson, CA 90745.

Deck vinyls. Like the antiskid floorings mentioned above but without the molded-in nonskid pattern, deck vinyls lay as easily as linoleum, look nautical, scrub clean easily, and wear like a bear's paw. Probably the best-known brand is time-honored Nautolex marine vinyl decking, which is still a good choice for areas on deck and below where a durable, salty, washable, quick-drying covering is needed.

It comes in wood and white planking styles, and in Marina, a deep-pile texture that looks like carpeting. Make your choices according to how much antiskid protection is needed in a given area. Often, combinations of surfaces are installed on decks, creating a pleasing pattern as well as adding antiskid protection in areas (such as the foredeck triangle) where they are needed most.

Tips on Choosing Carpet and Padding

• Natural jute or glued-on foam backings aren't recommended for marine use. Get a synthetic jute backing and padding that is recommended for yacht use.

• Any wall-to-wall carpeting should be installed by a professional, preferably one who is experienced in the marine field. Carpeting fresh from a dry warehouse, installed on a dry day, using a knee-kicker stretcher, may swell and ripple as it adapts to the damp marine environment. A professional may use a power stretcher, or may store the carpeting on the boat for a day or two beforehand to reach equilibrium, or both, to assure a taut finish.

• Natural fibers including silk, linen, wool, cotton, jute, and straw are likely to develop bad smells in a damp atmosphere. As a result, costly oriental rugs made of silk or wool aren't recommended except, in rare instances, for a boat that is always kept air conditioned and very dry.

• Some marine decorators prefer commercial-grade carpetings which are woven for extra-heavy wear. Because most boats have a set traffic pattern, one which can't be varied by rearranging furniture as one does at home, decorators go for tough, trackless, highly textured, low-sheen carpetings. According to the makers of Armstrong carpets, consumers name traffic laning as the most common cause of carpet failure, a bigger problem than staining. "You can have the best of both stain resistance and crush resistance," advises Armstrong.

• When choosing carpeting, take samples to your boat to see how colors look in that setting, in daylight and in lamplight.

• Give carpeting the "grin" test by bending a sample back to see how much of the backing shows through. The more backing you see, the less dense the pile.

• Fiber-optic technology is being designed into the carpeting of some of the most advanced yachts. Real strands of glass, which can transmit light, are actually woven into the carpet. They can be woven in randomly to add sparkle to the carpet or to lighten a dark passageway, or can be stitched into a pattern, such as a monogram or logo. The resulting light can even be programmed to track with the music system!

Carpet Care

- Request carpet-care directions from the carpet dealer or boat manufacturer and keep them on hand. A label may have been on the back of the carpeting, showing pattern number, style, and color name, and exact fibers. Keep a file of such information, any dated sales slips, and a record of dates when carpet cleaning equipment was used.
- Read warranties carefully. You may void a guarantee by installing carpeting wrong or by using the wrong cleaning process. Guarantees are usually just for the carpeting; you may not be reimbursed for removing the old or replacing the new.
- When removing old carpeting from your boat, do the job yourself if possible, and well in advance of the installation date of new carpeting. One reason is cost: Most installers charge as much for taking up old carpeting as for installing new. You'll save by ripping it out yourself. The second reason is that you may uncover rot or other problems that have to be dealt with before new carpeting goes down.
- Don't rely on old carpeting, after it has been removed, as a template for cutting new. If it had been stretched into place, it probably shrank after it was released.
- Vacuum as often as possible, using a vacuum cleaner with a beater bar. Never allow the vacuum bag to get more than half full.
- Spot-vacuum traffic areas at least once a day. Clean up crumbs right after meals, and immediately dry up any

It's important to vacuum around the table after each meal, and traffic lanes daily. Rechargeable vaccuum cleaners are always ready to use, even when you're away from the dock. Many models are available. BLACK & DECKER

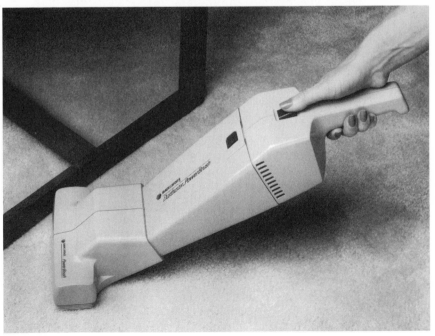

spills using clean paper or terry towels. Do not rub. See the stain treatment chart which follows. Don't be too quick to drench a stain with water, which could spread it, but do treat stains as soon as possible.

- Try to keep contact with salt water to a minimum. The water dries, leaving salt behind in the carpet. When dry, salt and sand abrade carpet fibers. Salt also absorbs moisture from the air, causing the rug to feel damp and sticky. Use good door mats, and get the crew in the habit of kicking off shoes before going below. Use water-based cleaning systems more often on a salt-water boat, to remove salt build-up.
- When using a steam cleaner on a carpeting treated with one of the new stainproofers, do not use a solution hotter than 130 degrees or the stain guard can be compromised. Don't set anything hot on these rugs.
- Almost all new carpeting sheds at first. Vacuum often.
- Most snags, pills, or "sprouts" should simply be cut off with scissors before they grow. Don't pull them out further. If a "run" develops, call in a professional.
- Avoid adding extra stainproofers, bug treatments, flea powders, and other chemicals to the carpet. They could damage finishes, dyes, or protectants.
- Beware of any iron or steel resting on your carpet. A common culprit is the protective glides or ferrules under furniture legs. They'll cause rust stains which are very stubborn.

Removing Carpet Stains

Although these instructions won't work every time on every stain, they are a good first line of defense unless your carpeting came with other directions. A professional cleaning, as soon as possible after your own treatment, is a good idea. Ammonia means clear, nonsudsing ammonia; vinegar means white vinegar; and detergent means a mild detergent that does not contain bleach, diluted with water at the rate of one teaspoon to one quart tepid water.

Solvent means a dry cleaning solvent. Caution: Many cleaning solvents are flammable.

Except in the case of acids that are eating into the carpeting, or dyes that are spreading and soaking in, it's best to scrape off and blot up as much of the stain as possible before beginning to work with water or neutralizers.

Mustard spills require special caution. Prepared mustard contains dyes which are so potent, any diluting will spread the stain. It should be left to dry, then scraped off.

When scraping spills off carpeting, don't rub. Scrape with a dull tool and lift toward the center of the stain, to avoid spreading the mess. Use as little liquid as possible, to avoid wetting the carpet backing and padding. Many modern carpetings are treated with antiwetting agents which keep liquids from soaking in.

Blot means to cover with a very thick (about one half inch) layer of paper towels or clean terry toweling. Weight them down, continuing the blotting and replacing with clean towels until no more moisture will wick into the towels. It's best to stay off the carpet until it is completely dry. Then vacuum or brush to restore the pile.

Take special precautions when using harsh chemicals around carpeting. There is no real cure for spilled oven cleaner, acne medication, chlorine bleach, tile cleaner, plant foods, battery acid, and other strong substances.

The final rinse is as important as the cleaning itself. Left behind, detergent residues will show up later as a telltale stain.

Stain Treatments

Greases, oily stains. Examples: petroleum jelly, tar, gravy and other greasy foods, butter, mayonnaise, paste wax, and ballpoint or felt-pen ink. Apply solvent, blot well, then wash with detergent. Blot, rinse, and blot.

Protein stains. Examples: egg, milk, blood, white glue, and fish scales. Dilute with detergent solution (cold if blood), blot, clean with ammonia, blot, rinse, and blot dry.

Lacquer, varnish. Clean with a solvent, then detergent solution. Rinse and blot.

Drinks. Examples: coffee, tea, juices, sodas, cocktails, beer, wine. Sponge with detergent solution, blot, then apply vinegar. Wash with detergent again, then blot, rinse, and blot again. If stain is stubborn, clean again with a dry cleaning solvent.

Dyes. Examples: oil-based paints, food coloring, furniture stains, fabric and hair dyes, bathroom chemicals, natural dyes found in some foods, and acne medications that contain benzoyl peroxide. See cleaning instructions for your carpeting. Sometimes only a professional carpet cleaner can help.

Rust. Use a commercial rust remover according to label directions, after testing on a part of the carpet that does not show. Sometimes detergent, followed by a vinegar rinse, works. Blot between each step, do a final water rinse, then blot dry.

Wax, chewing gum. Freeze with ice cubes, then hammer to break up into chunks. Vacuum fragments, then treat with dry-cleaning solvent, wait a few minutes while it works, blot, and use solvent again if necessary. An alternate treatment for wax is to scrape up as much as possible without damaging the carpet. Then cover the wax with several layers of paper toweling and iron with an iron set for silk. Avoid touching the carpet with the hot iron. Melted wax will soak into paper toweling.

Urine, vomit. Apply solvent and blot, then wash with water, blot, apply detergent solution, blot, rinse, and blot. The alkalinity of these stains varies. Sometimes ammonia will help, followed by thorough blotting, a wash with vinegar, another blotting, and a rinse. Then blot dry. Special treatments for such stains are sold in pet shops.

Acetone-soluble stains. Example: nail polish, some glues. Clean with a nonoily nail polish remover, blot, and repeat.

Dry powder stains. Example: chalk, soot, flour, nonfat dry milk. Vacuum immediately and thoroughly.

Battery acid. Sprinkle with baking soda and let it absorb as much as possible. Wearing rubber gloves, scrape up and discard where it can do no harm, then sponge with soda and water solution. Blot, rinse, blot. Call a professional to make repairs.

Disclaimer: the author makes no guarantees for these procedures. Cleaning technology is constantly changing. Get current information from the manufacturers of your carpeting. Additional advice may be available from the maker of the cleaning product, or from the maker of whatever substance caused the stain. Major carpet manufacturers have toll-free hotlines; keep yours handy. Avoid flammable solvents. Note that some cleaning procedures can void carpet warranties.

About Color Schemes

Color is today's decorator buzzword, and has become so important in everything from tiles to towels that groups of manufacturers often go together to coordinate a complete color wardrobe. Be sure to ask your carpet dealer or decorator if any dyed-to-match fabrics, linens, vinyls, tile, or other decorator products are offered.

Basic Carpet Cleaning Methods

Hot water extraction: Although this is one of the most effective cleaning methods, use it reluctantly on a boat, because soaking the subfloor may lead to rot. Hire a professional or rent a machine that forces hot water and detergent deep into the carpet. A special vacuum unit then removes the water. Drying takes days. High water temperatures could damage stainproofers.

Wet shampoo: A very popular method usually applied by rented or home machines, this is very tough on carpeting because the machine scrubs shampoo into the carpet with a rotary brush. Use it only as a last, desperate measure, and then only with great precaution to avoid soaking the subfloor. I do, however, keep carpet shampoo on hand (Star Brite makes a very good one for boat use) to use as a spot cleaner. By applying it sparingly, and using a soft bristle brush, you can avoid overscrubbing and excess soaking.

Foam aerosols. Sold in supermarkets, these spot cleaners are sprayed on, worked into the carpet with a cloth or sponge, and then left to dry. Residue is removed by vacuuming.

Dry powder extraction. The Host system is a rental machine that uses dry powder; Sears sells a system that relies on a powder called Capture. I've tried both, and they don't clean as thoroughly as wet methods, but they do leave a fresh look and smell, and are best for boat use. "Never use a wet carpet cleaner on a boat," advises decorator Vicky Moses. Although application is easier with one of the machines designed for dry powder extraction, the powders can also be sprinkled on by hand, worked in with a soft brush, then vacuumed according to manufacturer directions. The powders also work on most upholstery.

About vacuuming. Suction is better than sweeping, but the best job is done by a strong vacuum combined with beater brush action (which most lightweight and cordless vacuums do not have).

Free Booklets:

The Complete Book of Carpeting, DuPont Company, Room G-40284, Wilmington, DE 19898.

Understanding Carpet Quality, Armstrong World Industries, Consumer Response Center, Box 3001, Lancaster, PA 17604.

~~~~~~

Chapter 7

HUSH MONEY: NOISE-REDUCTION STRATEGY

~~~~~~

The sea is an unquiet friend and a raging enemy. Whether yours is a powerboat driven by hundreds of horses, or a sailboat with no engine at all, you already know that sound, much of it unwelcome, is a fact of boating life.

Underway there is the noise of engine(s), wind, and the rush of water. At rest, the boat is alive with nature's sounds: wind in the rigging, tides and currents chuckling under the transom, and the crackling of barnacles nestling on the hull. In addition, there are man-made sounds—pumps, compressors, the generator, hair blowers, drills, a stereo, and human voices.

At no time are such sounds louder than after bedtime in quiet anchorages, when you find that every move you make in your stateroom or head is broadcast loud and clear to everyone aboard.

The water itself carries sound, which travels readily through thin bulkheads and doors. And, operating in ways that you least expect, are channels that transmit sound between the most unlikely places. Heat ducts, ventilators, dorades, and even sometimes a bundle of electric wires can act as telegraphs to report your most private moments to everyone aboard.

Sound travels in odd ways on boats. My husband, Gordon, and I once spent a week aboard a ship on which we could hear every hiccup and whisper in the next cabin, even though the steady rumble of the engine gave us all the illusion that our voices were lost in the roar.

Another time on a sailboat in the Virgin Islands, one of our shipmates devoted much of the night to merry bouts of thumping infidelity on a hatch that was only a few inches above her cabin mate's face. What appears to be a secluded niche on deck may actually be a megaphone to some unexpected corner below.

Some of these areas can be staunched, stopped, or stuffed, but with others there isn't much you can do except to identify them and avoid them when you want to have a private row with your mate. Remember, too, that engine or generator noises which appear to mask sounds are not always working in your favor. Sounds carry differently. Voices, screaming to be heard over engine noise, may carry perfectly to areas where the engine isn't heard at all.

How can you make your yacht's living areas quieter, and your personal noisemaking more private?

Behind the Scenes

Within the boating industry, a variety of commercial products is used to deaden sound. Usually used lavishly in the engine and generator compartments, such materials are designed to do one thing: absorb sound. If you can find acoustic barriers which do more than one task, so much the better. For instance, Compositex, an Ozite product, is both a thermal acoustic material and a heat shield. New grommets and washers are available with sound dampening qualities.

In choosing a noise barrier for use behind the scenes, compare sound transmission specifications which are usually expressed according to ASTM-C423 (noise reduction coefficient) and ASTM-E336 (sound transmission class). Compare other specs, too, such as flame-spread index, oil resistance, water permeability, heat transfer, temperature tolerance, breaking or tensile strength, health hazards, and weight.

Ask if the product comes in other weights, forms, thicknesses, or densities. The more you can learn about the product's physical properties, the wiser choice you will make.

In addition, you'll want materials that are easy to install and that will stay put. Some must be bagged; some crumble when subjected to high engine room temperatures for long periods; some break down if they get so much as a whiff of fuel or oil. Fiberglass household insulation is a bad choice for boats because it's flimsy, and it holds moisture.

Some acoustic materials are soft, and can be bent around pipes or stuffed into voids. Others are rigid and must be cut to fit. Some are unfinished; some are finished on one side; some are finished on both sides. Sound-barrier materials aren't found in the usual outlets. Go to a boatbuilder, a company that does aircraft interiors, or industrial or automotive suppliers.

Boats have few areas that are right-angle square, but those that are square can be sound insulated with inexpensive, glue-on Styrofoam from home centers. It might work in some behind-the-scenes areas of your boat.

Styrofoam is available in various thicknesses. Thinner sheets insulate less but have a few degrees of "give" to fit mild curves. Unfaced Styrofoam isn't easily cleaned and it has minimal abrasion resistance, so its uses aboard will be limited and highly specialized.

Spray-on polyurethane foam can be useful in some spots, such as the area around the icebox or refrigerator. It deadens sound, increases insulation, and is waterproof. It comes out of the nozzle in a pleasant blob and flows readily into crevices and voids, and hardens to fit the space, so it's ideal for areas that you want to cover permanently (but not over wires, pipes, fasteners, or anything you want to see again). The only way to remove it is to cut, carve, and chop it away.

Soundproofing as Decor

First, have your mechanic and boat carpenter do everything possible to tame engine-room noise, then turn your attention to the boat's living areas. Much can be done simply by choosing one decorator touch over another. Here are some ways to soundproof at the same time you're furnishing or refurbishing the boat.

Take a survey of the boat underway, or at anchor with the generator running, to see what vibrations and noisemakers might be hushed. The stove is probably a major culprit, with rattles in the burners and oven racks.

Dishes, pots, and pans will ride more softly if they are stacked with coffee filters between. Cans and bottles will clank less in lockers if you slip the ribbed tops of old socks over them.

Take the occasional trip around the boat with a screwdriver and a spray can of lubricant, eliminating rattles and squeaks. To eliminate plumbing noise, install water hammers. Squealing joints can be shimmed.

Door hooks that are used to secure a door in the open position jangle annoyingly when the door is closed. Such hooks can be quieted by placing a patch of felt on the door. Or, replace hooks and eyes with friction latches.

Scan the boat to make note of where a softer, more sound-absorbing surface could be substituted for a hard finish. You'll probably be surprised at how many easy changes can be made. Replace parchment lamp shades with fabric shades, framed prints with tapestry or macramé wall hangings, and vinyl or aluminum blinds with fabric draperies. Wood cornices are out; padded fabric is quieter and is very "in" for cornices, wall panels, even overheads.

Cover switch plates with a fabric that matches draperies or throw pillows. In the head, replace the plastic shower curtain with a fabric one. Buy or make a heavy chenille lid cover for the toilet. Redo vinyl headboards with quilted fabric.

Thickly woven placemats are quieter than plastic ones, and a full tablecloth is quieter than placemats. Still available through the Vermont Country Store catalog (P.O. Box 3000, Manchester Ctr., VT 05255) is old-fashioned "silence" cloth, which quiets and protects the table.

Drawers, especially those that hold rattling items such as galleyware, tools, or cosmetics will be quieter if lined with sheet foam material. Large groups of small bottles will ride more quietly if they are pigeonholed (as in a spice holder) or grouped into cardboard or plastic boxes.

This book's sections on floor coverings and window treatments deal further with the sound-deadening virtues of plush textiles. If you're replacing headliners or hull liners, shop for the thickest, densest, most acoustically efficient materials. Nonwoven, marine carpet-type materials are made in thinner versions for headliner use. This is a plus to the decorator who is looking for an exact match between wallcoverings and floor coverings, to achieve a monochrome look.

These plush materials cover a multitude of sins, covering rough surfaces and absorbing sound in the bargain. Depending on the material, they are usually mildew resistant and fadeproof, and are moderately easy to clean (see below).

Perforated and solid vinyls are also made specifically for headliner use. They have a harder, shinier, colder look than fuzzy headliners, but this can be an advantage in dark areas where you want as much reflectance as possible. And vinyl headliners are easy to clean.

Because they are thin enough to telegraph underlying irregularities, plastic headliners require careful installation over a well-prepared surface, with appropriate beading and trim where needed. Proper adhesives should be used, to assure that the glue itself doesn't bleed through and stain.

Sheet cork looks good and is a time-honored insulator, but it holds moisture and crumbles if it mildews. I don't recommend it as a glue-on wall covering. However, inexpensive framed corkboards purchased from an office-supply house can be mounted on bulkheads and replaced easily if they mildew or rot. They're especially nice for areas where they can serve as bulletin boards, such as the chart room or a child's cabin. The larger and thicker the cork face, the more sound will be caught.

Cork-impregnated paints, which are used on some commercial vessels, are not recommended for yacht use because they're almost impossible to keep clean.

Rustiver is a deeply textured fiberglass "wallpaper" long popular in Europe where homeowners in centuries-old homes often use thick, forgiving wall coverings to cover damp, lumpy, old

Thickly textured fiberglass "wallpaper" can be used over old paint or irregular surfaces, then painted. 3G MERMET

walls. This material made by Mermet Corporation is extremely tolerant of temperature variations and dampness. It's washable, crackproof, nonflammable, and rot resistant.

Rustiver comes in white, in five different weaves and textures. It is glued to a wall and then painted. For information, write 3G Mermet Corp., 3965 Virginia Ave., Cincinnati, OH 45227.

Don't overlook the home-improvement market as a source for wall coverings to use aboard. Strong, deeply textured vinyls and fabrics can take lots of wear, scrubbing, and dampness. And, when it's time for a redo, they peel off in one piece.

Choices are endless, far more than the marketplace in marine materials. They include solid colors in a variety of textures from basketweave to grasscloth, subtle prints, and more extravagant prints in colors galore. Most designers also offer matching and coordinating borders, murals, and Scotchgard-treated fabrics.

Any of the adhesives and mildewcides designed for use in steamy bathrooms in the tropics can take the marine atmosphere. Don't shop discount stores. Get advice from a full-service paint and wallpaper outlet. You'll find a wide selection of wallpaper pastes, tile grouts, and other adhesives with mildewcides in them, and mildewcides that can be added by you, according to package directions, to other products such as paints or contact cements that you can't find in a mildew-fighter form.

About Condensation

Sea air is damp. Hulls are thin. Waters and winds are cold. When warm, moist cabin air hits a cold hull or deck, it begins to drip and dribble—feeding mildew, creating ugly stains, and making everything feel clammy. I've been awakened on cold mornings by frigid drops raining on my head from an overhead. Probably you have, too.

The right acoustical materials could also aid in the inevitable battle against condensation. The wrong ones could make things worse if they trap and hold moisture. Thanks to new textiles, plastics, closed-cell foams, synthetic carpeting paddings, and enclosed balsa-core materials, it's easier today than ever before to kill several birds with one stone.

The severity of your hull-sweating problems will depend on many variables including the thickness and conductivity of the hull, the humidity of cabin air, and temperature differentials, but it's likely you'll have at least some condensation, sometimes. If it settles in a spongy foam headliner and mildew gets a toehold, it's just a matter of time until the foam backing rots away and the headliner sags. There is no such thing as a boat that's too dry. Prepare for the worst, taking every moisture-fighting avenue you can think of.

Fight condensation three ways. First, cut down on dampness by stemming leaks, venting any heating devices, and using air conditioning if possible. Windows are a major source of condensation. Thin ones can be replaced with thicker or double-glazed windows. One source of thermal portlights is Sea-Glaze, 2340 Viscount Way, Richmond, B.C., Canada. Film-plastic solar window coatings also improve insulation somewhat. If possible, replace sweaty aluminum window frames with a less conductive plastic or wood.

Second, keep plenty of air moving through the boat, not just in living areas but in every corner of lockers and stowage areas. This can be done through adding vents to locker doors, replacing solid shelving with netting or slats, and perhaps adding a fan or dorade box here and there.

Third, choose materials recommended in this and other chapters to increase insulation without trapping moisture.

Cleaning Olefin Headliners

Amoco Fabrics and Fibers Company in Atlanta supplies the following instructions for cleaning their Amoweve wallcoverings. Thick, luxurious, and available in a wide choice of colors in various brand names including Polaris Plus, it's olefin backed in acrylic/latex. Tough, sound absorbing, abrasion resistant, stain resistant, and colorfast, it has the rich, textured look of the finest upholstery fabric. It's very popular with marine decorators.

First, recommends Amoco, it's important to clean stains early before they oxidize. Wet stains should be blotted or wiped off as much as possible with a clean, absorbent cloth. Dry materials should be brushed off as well as possible.

Then, try warm water first. If stronger action is needed, try powdered laundry detergent in water, or a carpet cleaner in water. Don't oversaturate; if the backing or adhesive get too wet, discolorations can bleed back through to the fabric.

Use a soft bristled brush, scrubbing from the outside of the stain toward the middle. Work up a mild lather and scrub in both directions to loosen the stain. Blot continuously as you go, to prevent saturation and dripping. Rinse with warm water and blot again.

Oil-based stains may be more difficult because they are chemically similar to olefin yarns. Start as above, adding a little bleach to the water. Again, take care not to oversaturate. Ammonia or vinegar can be tried but, with care, bleach should not harm olefin.

If the stain is solvent based, try the steps mentioned above before resorting to solvent cleaners. Use any solvents carefully and with plenty of ventilation, and use them sparingly so they don't penetrate the backing and damage it. Blot continuously during mild scrubbing.

For information about complete lines of noise-control materials for yachts, contact the Soundcoat Company, 1 Burt Dr., Deer Park, NY 11729. The company produces sound-absorbing, damping, and barrier materials in many configurations. At this writing, OSHA has not yet set sound-level limits for the marine field, but listed below, courtesy of Soundcoat, are limits that apply to merchant ships abroad.

Maximum Permissible Sound Levels

Location	West Germany dBA	Sweden dBA	Norway dBA	Denmark dBA
Machinery space without control room	90	85	90	90
Machinery space with control room	110	100	110	110
Machinery control room	—	70	75	75
Workshop	90	75	85	85
Storeroom	—	75	90	—
Wheelhouse	60	70	65	65
Bridge wings	65	70	70	70
Radio room	60	65	65	65
Office	—	—	65	65
Sleeping cabin	60	—	60	60
Dayroom	60	65	65	65
Saloon/smoke room	65	65	65	65
Recreation room	65	—	70	70
Recreation areas on deck	—	—	70	—
Working areas on deck and in cargo holds	—	65	—	—
Galley/pantry	—	65	70	70

A do-it-yourself engine-noise-reduction kit is available from Noise Reduction Enterprises, 6 Dodge St., Essex, MA 01929.

Hushcloth acoustical marine mat, a lead barrier material coupled with dual-density fiberglass, is available from BRD Noise and Vibration Control Inc., 112 Fairview Ave., Windgap, PA 18091. The company also makes a quilted blanket material consisting of a foam decoupler bonded to a vinyl barrier with a fiberglass absorber and a reinforced mylar facing. BRD offers complete lines of vibro insulators, vibration-control mountings, and specialized compression mountings.

Sonex decorative sound-insulator sheets are available from Illbruck, 3800 Washington Ave., N. Minneapolis, MN 55412.

One source for a self-adhesive, closed-cell foam sound insulator is Budget Marine, W. H. Den Ouden (U.S.A.) Inc., P.O. Box 8712, Baltimore, MD 21240. The company also sells sound-deadening floor and wall material, antireverberation plates, and sound-deadening plates.

Chapter 8

MORE ABOUT MATERIALS: LAMINATES, TILES, AND PLYWOODS

Decorative Laminates

Although many people persist in calling them all "Formica," the generic term is laminates, a long list of handsome, durable surfaces that will be basic necessities in any yacht remodeling or customizing project.

It all began in the early 1950s, with Formica's famous boomerang squiggle design, which has been making a comeback, thanks to the nostalgia boom. Since those early Formicas, the laminate world has exploded with new designs, colors, qualities, and applications. Stop thinking of laminates as just a countertop material. They can be used to cover bulkheads, to face cabinets and doors, to cover a workbench, and even to provide a static-free environment around electronics.

First, the colors. One company alone, Wilsonart, offers eight hundred and fifty different shades, allowing you to find an exact match for any color scheme. Among new patterns are imitation woods and marbles, stripes, checks, and linears. If you want dimension and texture to warm up a large, cold surface, choose laminates that are patterned like leather, basketweave, high gloss, pearlescent, matte, or denim.

Laminates are ideal for countertops in the galley and head, for splashboards around sinks, and for scorch protection around the stove. If you cover a bulkhead with laminate, it will be far more durable than paint, yet will take a fraction of the time to install. All you need is minimal surface preparation—far less than if you were priming and sanding for painting. Measure, cut, slather with adhesive, and slap it in.

Building in a cabinet or dresser? Face it with laminate. Can't afford solid teak for a door? Build it from plywood and face it with real teak laminate. Do you like the current trend toward the use of stonework, but don't want to add the weight? One new material has a thin face of real granite and a lightweight honeycomb backing. It sells for forty dollars per square foot.

Do you want the smart, new contoured look of rounded corners and flowing curves? Many laminates bend and conform. Do you dislike the ugly black edges that used to result where laminates joined? Get one of the new ones that is solid color all the way through. Looking for light transmission? Formica has introduced transluscent Alacore from Spain.

Any large building-supply store, and some decorators, can show you samples of the hundreds of laminates available. There are also full lines of metallics including aluminums, brasses, and coppers. Use a mirror laminate to brighten a dark forepeak, a copper to warm up a galley.

Add depth and interest by facing a surface in a corduroy laminate. Make a counter more skidproof by topping it with a deeply textured or pebbled laminate.

There are also deeply sculptured tambours, which are thick, woody laminates that are jointed so they can turn corners. Tambours can be used to fabricate disappearing locker doors, a rolltop navigator's desk, or built-in furniture with a wrap-around look.

So important have laminates become to today's yachts that one company, Advanced Technology Inc., offers hand-painted laminates in numbered and registered stock patterns and custom designs. Each sheet comes with a certificate of authenticity. The company is at 311 Regional Rd. S., Greensboro, NC 27409, telephone (919)668-0488.

Today's laminates are available in several thicknesses, from strong, structural materials to rigid sheets, to thin, very supple laminates.

Solid-core laminates such as Formica's Colorcore, which are the same color throughout, wear longer because the color and pattern won't scrub off. Used on countertops, they can take years of cleaning without wearing away the surface color. And, they can be turned into the most intricate moldings, cornices, built-in furniture, and galley treatments without concern over black joints.

A new development in edgings is a unique tongue-and-groove system that comes in conventional, bevel, and wood molding styles. One style, made with countertops in mind, extends a standard twenty-four-inch countertop an additional one and three-quarter inches to give a spacious, custom look. The new edgings come in colors and woods to match the entire Wilsonart laminate line.

On today's market you'll also find fire-rated laminates that comply with various codes, depending on how they are installed. Look into them for use around the galley stove or the fireplace in the saloon.

There are highly abrasion-resistant laminates, and chemical-resistant types, sold primarily to industry but which could be put on the workbench or on a vanity where cosmetics will be used.

One of the most beautiful new laminates is surfaced with real wood veneers in sixteen species from red oak to two mahoganies, a rosewood, and a teak. The product is cut and installed as easily as other laminates, then is stained and finished like any good wood. Like any laminate, of course, it should be used only in dry portions of the boat.

Working with Laminates

All laminates are not worked the same way, so apply according to manufacturer directions that come with each laminate you're using. Some "telegraph" patterns from a subsurface such as ply-wood grain, through to the finished surface. So, you may need a special subsurface.

Be sure to use the specific adhesive recommended for each laminate, too. Like laminates themselves, adhesives differ in their resistance to moisture, chemicals, and temperature, and in fire retardance. In the marine environment, these criteria are more important than ever.

General Rules

Laminates are for interior use and are not designed to endure standing water or harsh sunlight.

Most laminates are best cut and routed with carbide-tipped tools.

If you'll be using a lot of laminates in nonstandard sizes, look for a supplier who offers options. In addition to the usual 4' × 8' sheets, you can also find 5' × 8's, 5' × 16's, 4' × 12's, and custom cuts.

Most laminates are worked best at room temperatures (75 degrees; 45 percent humidity) and should be stored in this at-mosphere for at least twenty-four hours before work begins, to prevent expansion and contraction later. Any workspace should be clean, and free of paint spatters or any oily contamination.

An invaluable booklet, *Decorative Laminates for Architectural Surfaces,* describes laminates standards, adhesives, and codes, and is illustrated with ideas for unusual laminate applications. It's available from the Architectural Woodwork Institute, 2310 S. Walter Reed. Dr., Arlington, VA 22206.

If you want to know more about basic technical specs, (e.g., scuff resistance, wear cycles, postforming, fire retardance, dimen-sional change, et al.), they are published by the National Elec-trical Manufacturers Assn., 2101 L St. N.W., Washington, DC 20037. Send $10 for booklet LD-3.

The New Materials

Hard surface materials such as Corian, 2000X, and Avonite defy categorization. Generically, their manufacturers call them "solid structural material" or "solid, homogenous material." They look, work, and feel much like marble, and they are making an enormous splash with boatbuilders because of their ability to withstand tough wear. Although they are costly, and must be installed by specially trained technicians, they have a rich, regal look. Color goes through from front to back; it won't wear away with scrubbing.

Tiles

Although tile has never been the staple in American decor that it is in almost every other advanced nation of the world, tile use in the United States has doubled in the past five years. With its popularity ashore has come its increasing use on yachts, primarily in the galley and head.

Tile is trendy, versatile, nonflammable, fadeproof, hygienic, and is one of history's most ageless and durable products. The astute buyer will learn more about it, to make a wise choice for the intended project.

Although most of us just want to find the right size tile in the right color, tiles are also rated according to abrasion resistance, water absorption, surface crazing, frost damage resistance, dimension and color uniformity, electrical conductivity, warpage, bond strength, breaking strength, slip resistance, and thermal conductivity.

So, in addition to choosing color, shape, size, and pattern, you can also make use of special-purpose tiles which are, for example, more heat resistant for use around the fireplace or galley stove, more abrasion resistant when used as interior decking, more thermal conductive to make a passive solar collector, and so on.

Some manufacturers offer a line of tiles that are glazed with abrasives, for use as nonslip flooring. Although they're harder to clean, they also make for a more skidproof floor or galley counter.

Ceramic tile is an ageless material that has many uses aboard, both as a surface and as an accent. However, it's important to get the right tile and grout for each purpose, and to have tile installed by an expert. SUMMITVILLE TILE

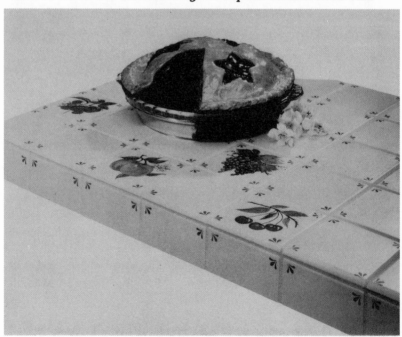

Durable new quartz and mineral glazes are best used in high-wear areas such as a head floor, or a galley counter in a charter yacht.

Tile is not the lightest-weight material you can use in any given application, so it shouldn't be used extensively on small boats, trimarans, racing boats, and other weight-critical vessels.

Even so, tiles are ideal as accents and trim, especially where hard wear or heat resistance are paramount. During a trip to Holland, Gordon and I carefully picked out a dozen Delft tiles and installed them around the two-burner Primus stove in our galley. We had already raised the boot stripe, and knew that our live-aboard essentials had burdened the boat beyond what her designers intended. Still, adding these few extra pounds brought us years of pleasure—and a scorchproof surface.

Types of Tiles

Nomenclature is confusing. In the United States, tiles under six square inches are called mosaic tile, larger sizes nonmosaic. Glazed nonmosaic is also called wall tile, and nonmosaic extruded glazed or nonglazed is called quarry tile. Dust-pressed glazed or unglazed nonmosaics are also called paver tiles.

The names of finishes are more self-descriptive. In the industry they are called clear, monochrome, mottled, faux (false marble, stone, slate), speckled, textured, bright, or matte. High-end tiles include silkscreened finishes priced at $4 or $5 each. In hand-painted tiles, you can spend as much as $5, $12, even $100 each.

While four-inch tiles are still common, and some decorators specify tiny mosaics, the trend is toward larger tiles with fewer grout joints, to create a more monolithic look. Foot-square tiles are available now, and eighteen-inch tiles are on the horizon. Smaller tiles mean more elaborate mosaics can be designed. Too, small tiles are easier to install on difficult areas such as a curved wall in the shower. However, larger tiles mean less grout to collect soap scum and mildew.

About Mortars and Grouts

There have been two significant developments in this area in recent years. One is the jump in the number of grout colors. A company that offered fifteen shades a few years ago now makes forty-seven colors, and grout is an important element in the overall look.

The other advance is liquid additives, to make Portland cement mortar faster setting, more flexible for bridging small cracks, or more suitable for special purposes such as setting marble. With the right formula, a tile installer can now build mortar up as much as three quarters of an inch without slumping.

These additives, known as latices or emulsions, are:

PVA. Polyvinyl acetate gives excellent bond strength, good resiliency, and fair color retention. It's highly water absorbent so is recommended only for use down below in dry areas.

SBR. Styrene Butadiene Rubber has good bond strength and resilience, fair color retention, and low water absorption. It can be used indoors or out.

Acrylic resin has excellent bond strength, resilience, and color retention, and low water absorption. It's used indoors and out.

Epoxy. Two-part epoxy emulsion and hardener, combined with a Portland cement sand blend have excellent bond strength, good resiliency, fair color retention, and low water absorption.

Used properly, such additives improve adhesion, tensile and flexural strength, eliminate voids or air pockets, inhibit water absorption, improve impact strength, and resist stains. And some are ultraviolet resistant, a plus for areas, such as trim around an on-deck spa, where sunlight would yellow conventional grouts.

Some yacht decorators scorn the use of tiles because they've had call-backs from previous installations in which grouts cracked. "Boats move and work," one decorator told me, "and grouts break loose." However, after talking to a Ceramic Tile Marketing Federation spokesman, and studying the full scope of available application materials, I'm convinced that a knowledgeable installer, working with modern grouts, won't have such failures, boat or no boat.

Buildings, too, expand and contract, and are usually subject to far more extreme temperature changes than boats are. Tiles are used widely aboard recreational vehicles, which move faster than most boats, and are also subject to vibration and twisting. Tiles, like most other materials mentioned in this book, can be considered in a twenty-first-century context.

For more information about the precise chemistry of Portland cement additives described above, order Bulletin 14 from the Materials and Methods Standards Association, 315 S. Hicks Rd., Palatine, IL 60067.

Sealers

Also new are clear, breathable sealers for grouts and tiles, to protect the finished surface from moisture intrusion, staining, and chemical damage. The new silicone sealers don't break down from ultraviolet and won't chalk. They protect both the tile and its bond, and won't break down as organic sealers do.

Tile Installation

Because tile must be put over the proper substrate, it's important to confer with your tile installer early in any tiling project. Plywood usually isn't suitable. Instead, use new backer boards which have waterproof membranes.

Used with the most water-resistant setting media, one fiberglass-faced gypsum board achieves permeability of .5 perms. Backer boards are now also available in lightweight 4' × 5' sheets, so you no longer have to wrestle with 4' × 8' sheets.

For more information, write the Ceramic Tile Marketing Federation, Suite 400, 1200 17th St. N.W., Washington, DC 20036. Telephone (800)426-TILE.

Plywoods

Almost every project aboard your boat begins with some form of plywood. It's used in cabinets, furniture, flooring, the workbench, shelving, countertops, and in almost every other area involved in any decorating or redecorating project.

Within the marine industry, many specialty plywoods are designed and laid up specifically for the harsh demands of the marine environment. To get less than the right stuff for the job, and to finish or seal it inadequately, is to ask for future disasters ranging from ugliness, mildew, and foul odors, to delamination and structural breakdown.

Keep in mind that there are hundreds of types and qualities of plywood. Not all woods dealt with in this section are marine-grade plywood, nor is marine ply necessary for many projects— nor are all marine plywoods adequate for all boat projects above and below the waterline.

The following standards have been set by the American Plywood Association. Many decorating projects aboard a boat can begin with inexpensive plywood, purchased from a local home center. Its success, however, will depend on your choosing the right ply for the purpose, and completing the project with proper marine adhesives, finishes, and sealers.

At the high end of the cost and beauty scale are specialty marine plywoods, faced with teak or mahogany. Because they are imported, they don't bear an APA rating, but brands such as Bruynzeel, which comes from Holland, have been tested extensively for both yacht and commercial ship use.

Complete construction, dimension, mechanical, fire, thermal, and other specs are available from the company, which sells a variety of materials including rubber inlay teak decking, marine plywoods including a mahogany, teak sole flooring, and decorative mahogany-veneer plywoods. Although such woods are costly, they are less expensive than solid woods.

Shopping for Plywood

Any time you're shopping for American-made plywood, look carefully at the ratings, which should be clearly painted on each 4' × 8' sheet. They will carry such designations as:

APA (indicating an American Plywood Association rating).

A,B,C,D (face veneer and back veneer, e.g., A-B indicates A face and B back; N grade means natural finish).

Thickness, e.g., ½".

Exposure durability class, e.g., Exterior, Exposure 1, Exposure 2, Interior.

Span Ratings. May read Rated Sheathing, Rated Siding, Rated Sturd-I-Floor, expressed in two numbers separated by a slash, e.g., $^{32}/_{16}$ or $^{48}/_{24}$. The first number indicates maximum spacing, in inches, of supports when used for roof sheathing with three or more supports. The second number stands for recommended spacing when the panel is used for subflooring. A panel marked $^{32}/_{16}$, then, may be used for roof sheathing over supports 32 inches on center or for subflooring over supports 16 inches on center. Such indicators are meaningful for the marine decorator who is concerned with strength of a subfloor, mattress base, or other load-bearing structure.

Group or Species Number

Group 1	Group 2	Group 3	Group 4	Group 5
Apitong	Cedar	Alder	Aspen	Basswood
Beech	Cypress	Red Birch	Cottonwood	Poplar
Tan Oak	Sweetgum	Redwood	Sugar Pine	

This is only a partial listing. For a complete list of these and other plywood specs, write the American Plywood Association, P.O. Box 11700, Tacoma, WA 98411. Information is also available from the Hardwood Plywood Manufacturers Association, 1825 Michael Faraday Dr., Reston, VA 22090.

APA Veneer Grades

A. Smooth, paintable, not more than eighteen neatly made repairs, made parallel to the grain.

B. Solid surface with shims, circular repair plugs, and tight knots to one inch permitted. Some minor splits allowed.

C. Plugged. Splits limited to ⅛" width, knotholes and borer holes limited to ¼" to ½". Admits some broken grain.

C. Tight knots to 1 ½", discoloration and sanding defects that do not impair strength. Limited splits, stitching permitted.

D. Knots and knotholes permitted to 2 ½" width, limited splits, stitching. Used only for interior, and Exposure 1 or 2.

CDX. An all-veneer sheathing, rated for Exposure 1, should be used only for limited exterior use.

Other indicators may refer to the mill number, product standard (usually PS 1–83 which refers to a United States Department of Commerce standard for construction and industrial plywood) and an FHA designation (which applies in Federal Housing Administration projects).

Specialty Panels

APA marine plywood is made only with Douglas fir or western larch, with solid jointed cores and highly restrictive limits on core gaps and face repairs. It can be used for hulls, is commonly available in thicknesses ranging from quarter-inch to three-quarter-inch, and is the best bet for any interior construction.

HDO: High Density Overlay panels are extremely abrasion resistant. HDO is a good designation for, say, a workbench.

MDO: Medium Density Overlay provides a good base for paint on both sides, for use in shelving, work surfaces, or built-ins.

APA Decorative: Rough sawn, brushed, grooved, or other decorative facing, available in exterior grades which vary according to the manufacturer. For use where a textured facing is needed.

APA Plyron: A plywood panel with a hardboard face on both sides. For cabinet doors, countertop, shelving.

About Treated Plywoods

Plywoods that are APA rated for exterior use have been glued with resorcinol or phenolic resins; interior components have used a casein glue with mold inhibitor. In addition to these ratings, various fire retardant and preservative treatments are available in the plywood industry. If you order these special woods and are concerned about load rating, be sure to ask about the rating of the treated wood. The treatment may have changed it.

Marine-Woods Suppliers

Bre Lumber, 10741 Carter Rd., Traverse City, MI 49684. Teak decking, marine plywoods, teaks, mahoganies. Bruynzeel imported woods; also source of Bruynzeel's Universal Edge Coating.

Boulter Plywood Corporation, 24 Broadway, Somerville, MA 02145. Large selection of decorative and structural marine plywoods, teak veneers, teak deckings, solid teak, mahogany.

Dean Hardwoods, Inc., P.O. Box 1595, Wilmington, NC 28402. Wholesale distributors of Burma/Thai teak, mahogany, afromosia, 500 board feet minimum.

East Teak, P.O. Box 322, Kirkland, WA 98033. U.S. West (800)537-3369; U.S. East (800)338-5636; Canada (800)228-1363. Teak, decking, lumber, plywood, and moldings. Minimum order $250.

Hartwood, Box 323 E. Golden Lane, New Oxford, PA 17350. Teak, mahogany, white oak, and other lumbers used in boat interiors.

Niedermeyer USA, P.O. Box 6737, Portland, OR 97228. Marine plywoods, cedar, spruce, bending white oak.

Wood Company, 4161 118th Ave. N., Clearwater, FL 34622. Wide choice of marine teak, mahogany, and plastic-faced plywoods.

~~~~~~

Chapter 9

DOOR TREATMENTS

~~~~~~

Why an entire section devoted to doors? Aboard your yacht, every door presents a large expanse of color, grain, or texture to the eye, for better or worse. Doors are among the easiest items to change or modify in a boat's interior, yet changing them can have a major effect for comparatively little labor.

Here are some possible scenarios.

The problem: More air circulation is needed.

Solutions: Marine stores and catalogs sell a large variety of metal louvers that can be placed in doors to provide venting with no loss of privacy. Or, make your own vent by cutting a small window in the door, then fill it in with a panel of caning, teak louvers, shirred fabric, or basketweave material.

Artistic slits or cutouts in a suitable motif can be cut in the door itself, to provide as much air exchange as possible between, say, a stateroom and its clothes locker. This looks best in a door that is solid wood; it's more difficult to get a clean, attractive cut in laminated doors.

Another choice is to replace solid doors with teak or mahogany doors that are fully or partially louvered. One company that specializes in marine doors is Happel Marine Inc., 474 Barnes Blvd., Rockledge, FL 32955. The firm makes a variety of louvered and half-louvered doors, and a basketweave teak that has a rich and exotic look.

The problem: Dark, solid doors give a closed-in feeling; you wish the cabin looked larger.

Solutions: Hang a full-length mirror on one or both sides. Or, put a mirror on the side where a mirror is needed (e.g., the stateroom) and, on the saloon side, a reflective surface that complements the decor but does not present a mirror image.

The problem: You want doors to transmit less sound.

Solutions: Many boat manufacturers upholster head doors on one or both sides with padded vinyl which looks good, cleans easily, and deadens sound. Add as much sound-absorbent material as you have room for. Then do a proper upholstery job, finished off with beadings and edgings.

A very simple way to upholster one or both sides of a door is by using Quik Trak, the plastic extrusion that is used to create instant, snap-in fabric panels. Use foam or batting behind the fabric, as a sound deadener. As an outer face, use vinyl or fabric. Because of Quik Trak's design, the material can be snapped out for laundering. The larger the panel, the better the sound insulation. For information about Quik Trak call (800)872-8725; address is 84 Reservoir Dr., Rockland, MA 02370.

In some situations, a thin door can be replaced with a thicker one, or with a sandwich core material that is no thicker but which transmits less sound. Look into acoustical barrier materials which can be glued between layers of wood or laminate.

In some boats, such as houseboats, areas are separated only by a curtain or by an accordion door that offers almost no sound insulation. Folding doors are sold in many thicknesses and qualities including real woods, so you may be able to upgrade to a closure that transmits less sound, closes more securely, and looks richer too. Ask at a home center to see samples of their accordion doors. Sears catalogs and home improvement centers offer premium-quality custom wood folding doors in a choice of finishes.

Also available are folding acoustical panels which are used in conference centers to create "break out" rooms. A commercial contractor who builds hotels or offices may be able to give you some tips on buying or building "disappearing walls" like these.

Doors between the boat's living areas and the engine room should have been fitted at the factory with a sound barrier which is chosen more for its acoustic properties than for its appearance. If you're getting too much engine noise, more sound insulation may be needed on the back side of this door.

The problem: The door blocks light.

Solutions: Marine manufacturers offer doors in clear glass or plastic, and wood doors with various light-transmitting panels.

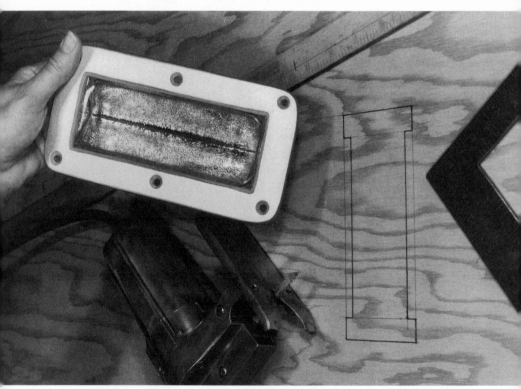

Deck prisms, available through marine catalog and chandlers, supply maximum light through minimum size. Where thickness allows, they can be installed in decks, doors, or bulkheads. GORDON GROENE

Entry and interior household doors, sold in home centers, have transparent and opaque lights in a galaxy of designs including elegant stained, beveled, and etched glass. Although they come in standard home-builder sizes, it's probable you can find a style that could be cut down to suit your needs.

Standard teak marine doors can be ordered with clear, dark gray, or bronze plexiglass inserts. The best place to begin shopping is with your boat's manufacturer, who may have doors in stock in standard sizes to fit openings in your boat, and in a material you want.

A simple, yachty way to transmit more light through a door, with no loss of privacy, is to install a deadlight or prism. Deck prisms are available through marine catalogs. Or, a craftsman who works in stained glass could design and fabricate a prism for your special needs.

The problem: The door lets in too much light.

Solutions: Sliding glass doors, most commonly found on sport-fishing boats and houseboats, present an enormous expanse of glass. This means more glare, more heat gain, less privacy. You may just need thicker, better-insulated draperies to close tightly across the doors. Consult a drapery expert who may design a multilayer window cover containing, for example, a layer that blocks heat and light, a filmy layer that blocks a little light but allows you to see out, and a conventional drapery layer that co-ordinates with the interior decor—all on their own tracks so they can be used singly or in combination.

Sliding glass doors usually have sliding screen doors. Replace conventional screening with one of the sun-filtering screens (Thermoscreen, Sunscreen).

Light-blocking films can be applied to glass doors. Some films filter only slightly, allowing an unrestricted view of the outdoors. Some block light more completely, but distort the view more. Some are a mirror finish, which allows people to see out but outsiders can't see in during the day. (At night, when lights are on inside, you'll still need draperies for privacy.)

The problem: The door takes up too much room.

Solutions: Replace a solid door with a two- or three-panel folding door or an accordion door. If space permits, consider putting in a pocket door, sliding door, or an articulated door that stows overhead or to one side (picture a rolltop desk). Laminate manufacturers offer tambour laminates in many textures and colors. They're popularly used for making roll-away galley locker doors but could also be used to make cabin doors or to close off a bunk.

Although fabrics don't make the best privacy barrier, they stow compactly, so a fabric door might be the answer for you. Make a curtain with two layers of heavy fabric, interfaced with as thick an interliner as can be managed. Devise ways to secure the curtain in both open and closed positions. A fabric "door" that installs with snaps can be removed completely, and stowed under a bunk cushion.

Where only a psychological privacy barrier is needed, a curtain of mosquito netting or other filmy fabric can be used to define a sleeping area. I once saw a master stateroom that was shared by a couple and their toddler, who had her own little sleeping nook. A curtain of gauzy netting surrounded the area to shield the child from the parents' reading lamps and to create a semblance of separation.

The problem: The boat has big, unappealing doors that you want to improve, without spending a fortune.

Solutions: If you're artistic, create a graphic design with boot-top tape. Or, add teak molding to create a paneled look. Or, for a daring high-tech look, shop the automotive aftermarket where you'll find dozens of self-adhesive trim strips in many shapes, in chromes and other metallics as well as colors, white, and black. Think up a dazzling design, and stick it on. One source of trim strips is Trim-Lok Inc., P.O. Box 437, Paramount, CA 90723.

If there is enough clearance in the door frame, glue a layer of a new, more exciting laminate over the existing one (see Laminates, p. 117).

Specialty wood suppliers (e.g., Woodworkers' Store, 21810 Industrial Blvd., Rogers, MN 55374) sell paper-thin teak, oak, mahogany, rosewood, and other fine wood veneers which can be glued over an existing surface. Just be sure first that it's satin smooth; irregularities will telegraph through.

The problem: the door is too heavy. Underway in rough seas, it's a handful. When you're sailing on one tack, the head door is almost impossible to open; on the other tack it takes a gorilla to close it. In rolling seas, a heavy door is a nuisance and sometimes a real danger.

The solution: The door that looked so stalwart and yachty in the showroom may not be the door that should go to sea with you. Consider a hollow or balsa-core replacement.

Chapter 10

LIGHTING THE WAY

Decorators know the value of light in bringing out a room's good points, minimizing its faults, expanding its size, raising a low ceiling, and creating any mood from bouncy and upbeat to mellow and romantic. Yet lighting is the most neglected accessory in boating, one which most of us yearn to correct from the first night spent on board.

A harsh light aimed the wrong way can magnify irregularities in the most exacting joinerwork or overhead. It can shine uncomfortably in one's eyes, or can light up corners you wished you had cleaned more carefully. Lighting that is too strong can cause hot spots on upholstery or draperies, can drain batteries, can keep bunkmates awake while you read yourself to sleep.

Where lights are too dim, you can't find an elusive lemon deep in the ice chest, or you stumble over a step in a companionway, or you can't make out the fine print in the coast pilot.

Because living areas in most boats are meant to be used for more than one purpose, it's important that lighting match those multiple uses. For example, lighting at the table should be subtle enough to enhance an elegant dinner. Yet, when you want to use that table to play cards or to knead bread, brighter lighting is needed. And, when that table is made into a bunk, guests should be able to read comfortably after they turn in.

Aboard many yachts, the chart table doubles as counter space in a galley or as a wet bar. Different lights will be needed for planning a course by day, another for chart work and making log entries underway after dark when you must protect your night vision, and another for bartending at anchor. In the saloon, you probably want subtle and flattering lighting for relaxed conversation, and brighter, better-aimed lights for reading.

When amps are plentiful, light up to beat the band. When you're dockside or are on generator power, enjoy all the advantages of 110V household lighting. When you're on short wattage rations, use lamps that give the most bang for the 12-volt buck. In steamy climates, you want lights that burn cool. In winter, the heat of an Aladdin kerosene lamp adds a warm and cozy halo to the cabin.

There are many ways to light your boat. The more variety and redundancy, the better.

About Lights

Although we're all familiar with the use of wattage in determining a bulb's strength, that term refers only to the amount of electricity it uses. Other factors are important. One is the bulb's efficiency, expressed in lumens. One lumen is the amount of light that falls on one square foot, at a distance of twelve inches from a candle flame. Fluorescent lights produce more lumens per watt, and can therefore be considered more efficient.

The second factor is bulb life, which is expressed in hours on the bulb package. If a light fixture is very awkward to get at when a bulb must be changed, long bulb life becomes as important, perhaps more so, than efficiency or light quality.

Quality of light is another important consideration. It determines how accurately you can read a colored chart, how healthy your complexion will look at the dinner table, and how well you're setting the scene for romance in the master stateroom.

Incandescent bulbs, which give out a mellow tone rich in reds, are a good choice for flattery, and "soft white" bulbs may be even better because they diffuse light more. Incandescents, however, use more wattage and have a shorter life than fluorescents.

Although most of us have at least some fluorescent bulbs at home, the layman doesn't know—and usually doesn't need to know—about the many types of bulbs available. Yet lighting experts know that chromacity is a vital consideration in choosing a bulb for any color-critical spot such as a retail store, restaurant, intensive-care unit, or a museum.

Expressed in kelvins, chromacity ranges from low numbers that are warm reds and yellows and climb into higher numbers that express cooler blues and greens. Where one bulb is right for a meat inspection lab, it would be wrong for a jewelry store; right for the galley, wrong for the bedside.

That's why companies such as General Electric and Westinghouse offer an enormous choice of bulbs to fit incandescent, fluorescent, and HID (high intensity discharge) lamps. To the yacht decorator, it means the opportunity to warm up or cool down a space. By choosing the right bulb, you can provide a strictly neutral, nondistorting light in areas where discerning color is important (such as sorting the black socks from the navy blue) and good, bright light for areas where you're reading or doing chart work.

According to GE, the color of a light source does not affect productivity or the ability to do black-on-white seeing tasks, but the company points to studies at Ohio State University showing that people, especially older people, do perform better as lighting levels increase—regardless of whether the light is cool or "warm."

So, for reading, chart work, and peeling potatoes, you want quantity rather than quality. In decorating, however, quality of light is an important tool you can use at no extra cost in either dollars or wattage.

If you want to go more deeply into chromatics, write General Electric, Nela Park, Cleveland, OH 44112 and ask for Bulletin 905-61701R which contains a complete, highly technical chart of lamp color specifications.

Or, see a lighting specialist who can help choose the right bulbs for efficiency, the best color rendition, and for special purposes such as diffused or shielded light. For example, GE's SP35 bulb is toward the low (warm) end of the kelvin scale, issuing a pale

yellowish light that enhances reds, oranges, and greens and sub-
dues deep reds. Their **SPX27** and **WWX** fluorescent bulbs are
said to be the best simulation for incandescent light. An artist who
wants the best simulation of a clear north skylight would choose
a **C75**.

The bulb you choose to shine bare will be different from the
bulb you place behind a cornice, louver, or diffuser. The options
are enormous, confusing, and very exciting. They are also important to your yacht's look, to creating more appealing and
cleaner meals in a better-lit galley, and to navigation safety.

How Light Reacts with Color

Color Rendition	Incandescent Fluorescent and Soft White	Fluorescent Standard Cool White
Appearance on neutral surface	Yellowish-white	White
Effect on atmosphere	Warm	Cool
Colors enhanced	Red, orange, yellow	Green, yellow, blue
Colors grayed	Blue	Red, orange
Complexion	Enhanced	Grayed

Table courtesy of GE

How Much Light?

Light Source	Watts	Lumen Output*
Fluorescent light stick	33	725
Soft-white fluorescent	40	2150
Circular fluorescent	44	1750
Soft-white energy-sparing incandescent	55	855
Soft-white incandescent	60	855

*Varies from manufacturer to manufacturer
Table courtesy GE

Most boats today are fitted with combination 12V and 110V
light fixtures. The first step in redoing your yacht's lighting is to

know what wiring is available where, and how difficult it will be to add more where you want it. *Your Boat's Electrical System*, by Conrad Miller and Elbert Maloney (Hearst Marine Books), contains chapters on how to add AC and DC outlets to a boat, and is an invaluable reference if you'll be doing the work yourself. If not, get a qualified *marine* electrician.

Some lights can be added, some changed, and others simply shielded, recessed, designed to deliver indirect light, or reduced in wattage. First, evaluate your needs, then study the market-place—marine stores, marine catalogs, household electrical suppliers, home stores, RV and camp stores, and specialty catalogs. You'll be surprised and delighted at the options available.

Take a Lighting Inventory

It isn't until darkness falls that you find where your yacht's lighting falls short, so take notebook in hand and walk through the boat after dark, noting problem areas. Lie down on bunks and try the reading lights in both AC and DC modes. See if you can find switches in the dark.

Turn on various lights, to see if it's possible to create environments in which you would be comfortable reading, watching TV, conversing with guests, trimming green beans at the galley sink, or listening to music on the stereo. Try it with the 110V system, and again using only the 12V lights.

Work with a friend, and observe what happens, under different lights, to the color of his or her complexion, wrinkles, hollows under the eyes. Just as candlelight softens the look and lights the face from below, overhead lights cast shadows under the eyes. And, if those lights are fluorescent, they give the skin a sickly blue hue.

Keep in mind that blackout lighting (i.e., the kind of green or red lights used in photography darkrooms or airplane cockpits) may be needed in the galley, head, nav station, and perhaps other critical areas where light must be available and yet must not be allowed to disrupt the helmsman's night vision.

Go through this list, making notes about whether the lights to be added should be 12V, 110V, or both; incandescent or fluorescent; bright or merely moody.

Saloon
————Reading lamps
————Low light for conversation, TV, listening
————Lighting for specialty areas such as stereo center,
VCR, bar, over card table, any stowage areas
————Reading lights suitable for those sleeping in
sofabed

Head (repeat for each head)
————Shaving/makeup
————Blackout lighting
————Nightlight
————110V outlet for hair blower, curlers, shavers, electric toothbrush
————Toilet area
————Shower area
————Stowage area(s)

Chart Station
————Chart light
————Lights needed to operate any equipment
————Lights needed for other purposes this area?
————Blackout light

Galley
————Light over sink
————Light/blower over stove
————Counter areas/work areas
————Stowage areas
————110V outlets for appliances
————Refrigerator/icebox
————Oven cavity
————Reading/work light, galley table
————Mood lighting, table area
————Reading lights suitable for those sleeping in convertible dinette bed
————Blackout light(s)

Cabin (repeat for each cabin)

————Reading in bed

————Makeup, grooming

————Clothes locker(s)

————Overhead fixtures to light drawers, stowage areas

Engine room

————Portable trouble light, reaching all areas

————Workbench

————Engine(s)

————Generator

————Outlets for tools

Other

————Minilight floor lighting along passageways

————Footman lights at spots where footing is tricky

————Track lighting

————Highlighters for artworks

————Lockers not included above

————Stowage areas not included above

Some Lighting Terms and Tricks

Aircraft-style lights. They can be aimed with pinpoint accuracy and are available from the *12 Volt Catalog* (see Chapter 14).

Cornice lighting. Downlighting used under a cornice. *Valance lighting* is placed behind a cornice, and directed both up and down. *Canopy lighting* shines upward from a cornice, or canopy, and reflects evenly back into the room from the ceiling. *Soffit lighting* is placed under a diffuser, usually over a galley workspace, a desk, or a makeup table. In *cove lighting,* a saloon is surrounded by a cove molding with lights evenly placed behind it, lighting only the overhead.

Eyeball fixture. A recessed round light that can be aimed at a painting or fixture.

Fiber-optic lights. No longer mere gimmicks, these versatile new lights may have a place in your lighting scheme. These lights can turn corners, and they provide a lot of illumination for scant wattage. Fiber-optics might, for example, be used in emergency lighting that points a pathway or outlines an emergency switch, or in areas where light is needed in a dark corner.

Floor can. An upward-directed spotlight to place in corners or behind plants, shining on a bulkhead to light a cabin indirectly.

Open downlight. An open bulb light that aims at a task or accent site. Don't use it over a shiny area, such as a table top, where it will cause glare.

Projector spot. A long, narrow beam to throw light on a small area from a long distance. Good as a modeling effect. A "framing" projector spot shapes a beam to fit a precise area, such as a tabletop. New shallow profile recessed spots are ideal for boats because they are more compact.

Track lighting. Long popular in homes and commercial buildings, track lights are enormously useful in boating because they come in so many types and sizes for the many different requirements of multipurpose areas of the boat. With only one electrical outlet, you can operate reading lights, mood and modeling lights, and even a small fan. Get lights with individual off-on switches; you'll probably use different lights at different times.

Tube lighting. Decorator Vicky Moses of Oceanic Designs makes effective use of enclosed 12V "strip" lights in which many small bulbs are strung inside a protective tube. Rigid tubes are available in almost any length to mount overhead, on a bulkhead, under a cabinet, or along a dark passageway. Flexible tubes can be used to outline an area such as a cornice or lambrequin. Tube lights are sold by automotive and RV suppliers; RGM Industries, 3342 Lillian Blvd. Titusville, FL, 32780 telephone (407)269-4720, specializes in marine-quality tube lights which have replaceable bulbs.

Quick-disconnect chandelier fitting. Now sold in electrical supply stores, these special fittings allow quick, twist-off removal and unplugging of a chandelier so it can be stowed safely before getting underway.

Wall Washer. Bathes a wall with even light. Can be an effective way of indirectly lighting a cabin.

Waterproof lights. Sold for use on deck and in wet passageways, waterproof 12V/110V lights can also be installed in the shower. An efficient, sealed light with a Fresnel lens is offered by West Marine Products.

Nonelectrical Lighting

Mellow and glowing, kerosene lamps and candles paint the cabin with soft, lively, flattering light. Besides being lovely and traditional, such lights are practical because they're there when you need them in times of electrical failure or shortage. One of the best selections of imported, solid brass kerosene lamps designed for yachts is carried by West Marine Products, P.O. Box 1020, Watsonville, CA 95077. Write for a free catalog.

Most kerosene lamps have wicks, and there are also brass lamps which are used with special, dripless candles. A third choice is a mantle-style lamp in which a very delicate fabric mantle burns with an intense, hot, white light. Coleman's classic gasoline lantern is an example of this type lamp. Aladdin makes a large choice of kerosene mantle-type lamps in elaborate decorator styles as well as traditional brass models.

Other choices to consider as backup, emergency lights include battery lamps, shielded candles, and propane lanterns. Good selections in attractive styles are sold in camping supply stores and catalogs.

On our boats we also carry a supply of Cyalume chemical light sticks. Although they have to be replaced as their shelf life expires, these sticks are waterproof and flameproof to provide emergency light when all else fails.

Chapter 11

~~~~~~

FURNITURE

~~~~~~

"Furniture for a yacht has to be scaled down, not just to save space but for visual impact," says Bob Gillespie of Hutton Furniture. The firm's Boatable line, much of it sold to boat builders to furnish new boats, is designed specifically for marine use. "Even aboard the largest yacht, the saloon will be downsize. Furniture must be in proportion," he says.

"We find many boat owners are tearing out their built-ins and replacing them with real furniture," Gillespie reveals. "Built-ins are usually flat, have no pitch, and are uncomfortable."

The company makes sofas, chairs, and coffee tables that look like, and are as comfortable as, household furniture. But they cost more, have better endurance, and make every inch of space work overtime. Hutton's manufacturing guidelines make good sense, whether you're buying their furniture or are building or ordering your own.

The company makes sofas in many sizes, all available with either under-seat stowage bins or a pullout bed. Glen Eagle, another specialist in yacht furniture, offers optional fishing pole storage under its sofas. Chairs, too, are available with under-seat storage. I sat comfortably on a Hutton sofa to interview Gillespie, not realizing until he pointed it out to me that the seat was a few inches narrower and the back lower than a household piece.

A variety of its treatments is shown here in the display that Aqua Marine takes to boat shows. Note the use of rounded corners, quilted fabrics, blinds, and valances.
AQUA MARINE

Fabrics are Scotchgard treated. "Some other treatments cause seam slippage or color bleeding," warns Gillespie. "Stick to a name-brand fabric coating."

The lightest suitable hardwoods are used for Hutton frames, to keep weight at a minimum. Metal springs are eliminated with the use of strapping and foam cushions. Zippers, buttons, and leg glides are rustproof nylon. "Metal buttons under furniture legs will cause rust stains on carpeting," Gillespie finds. "Avoid them."

Gillespie likes rounded corners, and so does Bud Pettisani of Aqua Marine Products in Vineland, New Jersey. For one thing, the rounded look is in style. For another, rounded corners are safer on a boat underway. And, says Pettisani, a little barrel chair can be tucked into odd corners of the boat that couldn't accommodate square chairs.

146

First Impressions spokesman Jeff Smith told me his entire line is custom-made including whatever mechanical, hydraulic, or electronic activators are required. The company's hi-lo hydraulic table is pushbutton activated, not only rising and lowering but changing angles so the legroom is correct in both positions.

One client wanted a backgammon board that would fold out of a wall. Another wanted a complete disco, including a fiber-optic dance floor, on his eighty-five-foot Hatteras.

One of Smith's most popular options is a rotating media column that contains all the saloon's entertainment electronics—television, VCR, CD player, and such. With the touch of a button, it rotates 180 degrees and turns its "face" to the bulkhead, presenting only a smooth column to the saloon. It's a security measure, hiding the electronics when they aren't in use, and it looks better than having an unused TV staring into the room.

First Impressions does the media column electronically for ten

This wooden game table has a flat surface, and a recessed game board with magnetic chess and checker games. Cutout areas hold accessories and drinks. The table is solid oak. OEM Supply Inc., 50340 Faith Ave., Elkhart, IN 46514.
OEM SUPPLY INC.

thousand dollars. A manual version, which they put in a sixty-footer, is less. One of Smith's greatest coups is an underwater camera that televises the bottom and shows it, to the lucky folks aboard an eighty-five-foot Hatteras, on a monitor built into the cocktail table.

I've cruised aboard two boats that had underwater viewing, one through a portlight on the floor of the master stateroom and another that had a glass viewing port in the hull under the galley table. If you'll be cruising coral waters, I guarantee that underwater viewing will be the most popular of any entertainments you could provide.

At Cruisers Inc., the look can be elegant without forgetting yachty practicality. The company may, for instance, use clear acrylic fiddles for a protective rim, which their decorators believe have a "clean monochromatic" look but which are still useful, durable fiddles.

Leathers, suedes, and man-made suedes have become as important afloat as they are to decorators ashore. However, "Don't take residential leather furniture to sea," cautions Hutton's Gillespie. "It won't hold up to the temperature extremes and other hardships." Make sure you get leather that is tanned and treated for harsh use. If you can't find a marine supplier, get automotive leather.

A clever touch used aboard the *Kathleen W,* a corporate party yacht available for charter out of Fort Lauderdale, is clear acrylic chairs. They become almost invisible against the background, making the lounge and saloon seem far more spacious. One bulkhead is covered with an etched mirror, which ads an illusion of space and light without the added motion and visual confusion that are created by too much mirroring.

Clear acrylic is available now in so many thicknesses and sizes, it can be used to fabricate anything from a galley table to end tables, "room" dividers, and pass-throughs. Look in the telephone yellow pages under Plastics. Then work with a professional who is well versed in how to cut, edge, fasten, and protect clear plastics.

One more tip, from decorator Vicky Moses: "Keep weights and center of gravity in mind. Some household-type pieces are

Note how the clear, acrylic chairs disappear in the saloon of the charter yacht Kathleen W, *making a small area seem far more spacious.* WINDRIDGE YACHT CHARTERS

well suited for yacht use in every way except they are top heavy and tip too easily."

Pedestal tables are among the biggest culprits. Even those that have a wide footprint can, if they have very heavy tops such as marble or plate glass, get going like pendulums in a rolling boat. Floor lamps, too, even those that are perfectly balanced for use in a house, can topple in a rolling boat.

I was once having dinner aboard a yachty houseboat in the Hudson River when a bit of a sea came up and the plush dining chairs, which had ball rollers, began traveling. Large ball rollers, in boats with thick rugs, usually aren't a problem but it wouldn't be wise to use them on anything but the most tame and predictable waterways.

Built-ins Versus Free-Standing

Only a generation ago, free-standing furniture was rare on all but the largest yachts. Today it is much more popular, even on smaller boats. If you're doing a rip-out remodeling, or are ordering a custom boat from a bare hull, and have the luxury of choice, here are things to consider.

Built-ins
Pros

- Anchored with absolute security
- Makes optimum use of every available millimeter of floor space
- Exploits every possible stowage opportunity
- Can be styled precisely to yacht's look

Cons

- Can't be removed easily from boat for cleaning, painting
- Floor plan can't be changed
- Often not engineered for optimum comfort when sitting, sleeping, dining

Free-Standing Furniture
Pros

- Looks more homelike
- Individual components can be changed and rearranged to suit occasion, or change wear patterns on carpeting, or create new look
- Individual pieces easily replaced when worn; complete redo not necessary
- Can be removed from boat for cleaning, reupholstery, boat maintenance

- Many household pieces suitable, and available at home-furniture prices

Cons

- May break loose in rough seas
- Fewer choices than with custom built-ins
- Costs more than comparable household pieces
- If purchased from a furniture store, may have hidden drawbacks such as steel parts that will eventually rust and bleed through
- Offers no stowage compartments

Deck Furniture

In large cities, entire stores are devoted to patio furniture. Although many styles and materials are unsuitable for deck use, there is an enormous choice among wicker, enameled tubular aluminum, rattan, woods, steel, wrought iron and plastics. Some stores specialize solely in PVC (polyvinyl-chloride) furniture made from plumbing pipe.

Both the Sears and J. C. Penney catalogs offer outdoor furniture, some of it seaworthy. In season, outdoor furniture is also displayed in home centers, discount stores, pool suppliers, and department stores. Marine stores and catalogs usually carry at least some deck furniture, such as folding director's chairs. Through boating catalogs, good selections of solid-teak deck furniture, with all-brass hardware, are available.

In addition to suitable style and color, decisions to be made include:

Stowable versus rigid. Large, enclosed aft decks are often furnished permanently with porch furniture. Consider, however, whether you'll ever have to stow the furniture. Underway in heavy weather, for instance, it will have to be anchored or stowed. And you may want to stash it somewhere at times to make room for big, stand-up parties.

Even if you opt for noncollapsible furniture, have some folding chairs available for extra guests. It's hard to improve on teak

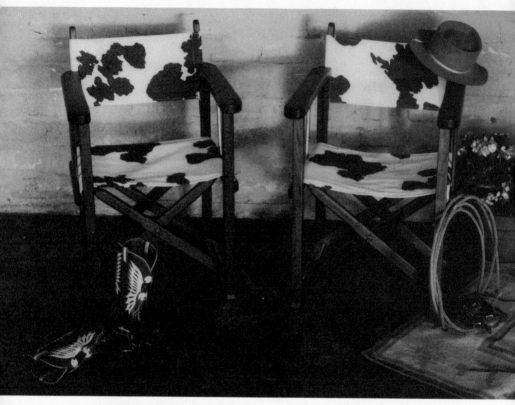

Folding campaign chairs can be used on deck and below. A prestige line by Santa Barbara Designs (P.O. Box 90610, Santa Barbara, CA 93190) comes in hand-rubbed teak, natural silver patina, or sunwashed, with fabrics in a choice of ninety-five colors, prints, and stripes.

directors' chairs with brass hardware, and folding teak deck chaises styled after those used on ocean liners in the 1930s. Both are sold through marine catalogs and stores.

Type of padding or upholstery. Woven plastic chair and chaise pads are thick and cushy enough to pass as fabric, yet they drain dry quickly after a rain. They're sold in standard sizes in patio stores. Marine-grade coated canvas fabrics are a good choice for custom upholstery, but most of them are not completely waterproof. They should be put on over some waterproof stuffing, such as closed-cell foam, which cannot become saturated.

Avoid cheap, plastic, readymade pads, which break down

quickly from sun damage and soaking. Replacement covers for directors' chairs should be made from a good marine canvas, preferably one treated for water and ultraviolet resistance.

The choice of marine vinyls has never been better, and there is no more practical material for deck upholstery. Still, there will be places where you'll prefer the look and feel of fabric. A compromise, if you're having deck furniture custom upholstered, is to have fabric on one side and vinyl on the other, or to cover vinyl cushions with marine canvas slipcovers.

Marine versus household. Almost always, furniture bought from marine stores costs more than that bought from discount houses. Often, the extra cost is justified because it means brass and stainless-steel hinges and screws rather than steel, or a heavier enamel coating, or better anodizing, or a better grade of canvas upholstery, or a downsizing that is more in proportion to yacht dimensions.

Other times, however, discount furniture is ideal for deck use. Rubbermaid makes stackable, all-plastic chairs for outdoor use. They're so sturdy and sunproof, they're used by many resorts and by houseboat rental fleets.

J. C. Penney's catalog offers solid cherry, Scandinavian-style folding wood furniture that is said to have no metal fasteners. Pipe furniture is pipe furniture, plastic through and through. It's bulky compared to some styles, but it's almost indestructible.

If you're in doubt about whether deck-chair fasteners are solid brass or plated, test with a magnet. If they are ferrous, but are a standard style and size, you may be able to replace them with stainless. If the piece has steel feet, remove or replace them at once or they'll make rust stains on deck. Where possible, add sturdy rubber crutch tips to furniture legs, to make them less tippy underway.

If you haven't room to install a marine fireplace, look into freestanding portables. They are independent units requiring no venting or surrounding insulation, and burn a solid alcohol fuel under a log-look insert. Use one on deck or in the saloon, and take it home between cruises. Portable fireplaces are available through specialty catalogs, recreational vehicle suppliers, and J. C. Penney.

Upholstery Cleaning Codes

Request fabric cleaning codes from your boat manufacturer, fabric supplier, or furniture maker and take care of all fabrics accordingly. Codes include:

W: Can be washed with a water-based cleaner.

S: Clean only with pure solvents.

SW: Use either a water-based or pure solvent cleaner.

X: Vacuum only.

For more information:

Glen Eagle Furniture, Statesville, NC 28677, (704)873-3244.

Hutton Furniture Company, P.O. Box 158, Hickory, NC 28603, (704)322-3330.

Chapter 12

~~~~~~

ELECTRONIC PLEASURES

~~~~~~

A sophisticated electronic entertainment center is as much a part of the living area in today's yacht as GPS and Loran are in the navigator's station. No longer do we have to settle for crackling AM stations, pulled in by the RDF when conditions are right. As a minimum, you'll probably have a good stereo system wired for sound throughout the boat. Beyond that, the sky's the limit.

There are a few major differences between electronics you'll use on your boat and those chosen for the home. First is your cruising area. Second is the damp, corrosive marine environment. Third are space limitations, both for the equipment itself and for storage of your tape, CD, or video library. And, of course, it's a plus if everything runs on battery power so you don't have to run a big generator just to watch TV.

Changes in electronics have come so thick and fast, most consumers don't know which way to look. VHS clobbered Beta; LP records have disappeared from the stores; eight-track is ancient history; DAT may blow CD out of the water; cable TV may be available through telephone lines at every dock.

The marketplace offers a big selection of compact color and black-and-white televisions in AC/DC, battery, or AC power, with other features such as radio, alarm clock, remote control, or VCR. Some are meant to be shelf-mounted; others hang up. Buy one with mounts and controls suitable to your needs. SONY

Sony's mini sound system takes little space, but includes CD player, AM/FM tuner, dual cassette deck, remote control, and three bookshelf speakers. SONY

Sony's compact, water-resistant speaker is an ideal companion for a Walkman or Discman. The amplifier works on internal or external batteries, or 110V power. SONY

Full-feature tape players are available from companies that specialize in electronics for the marine environment. SI-TEX

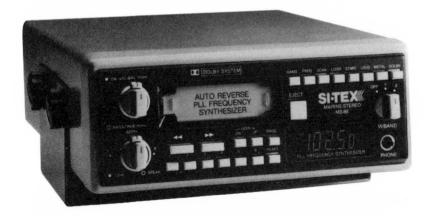

A five-in-one laser disc player from Sharp has a multi-changer for 3" and 5" formats, and also plays 8" and 12" laser discs, 3" and 5" CD's, and 5" CD videos. SHARP

Sharp's portable VCR television combination works on household power or internal or external batteries. SHARP

The farther you cruise from your favorite FM station, the more important it is to have a good CD/ tape player. SHARP

New television choices include LCD screens only an inch thick. SHARP

Consider the Source

If you'll be ranging worldwide, in and out of reception areas, you'll be relying more heavily on your own audio and video library than if you spend most of your time tied up at a marina which has cable TV, or do all your cruising within reach of your favorite FM jazz station (usual range up to fifty miles).

Technology is changing rapidly but, for now, satellite dish reception is not practical or affordable for a moving platform such as a boat underway or even at anchor. So for television, you'll probably rely on cable, whatever local stations you can receive, or videotapes.

Very good TV antennas are available through boat and camping suppliers. Some are permanently mounted in a weatherproof housing; others recess when not in use; still others dismount for easy stowage. Many of those sold for use on boats or recreational vehicles have a remote control that allows reaiming from down below as the boat swings at anchor.

The Marine Environment

The more exposed the equipment, the more important it is to get marine-quality equipment and to install it according to the best and most protective marine techniques. An excellent guidebook is *Your Boat's Electrical System,* by Conrad Miller and Elbert Maloney (Hearst Marine Books). Although it devotes very little space to consumer electronics *per se,* it's the basic bible of marine electrical systems and electronics.

In choosing equipment, remember that many euphemisms are in use. Terms such as water resistant, splashproof, heavy-duty, or impact resistant could mean almost anything. Other terms, such as waterproof, underwater, or submersible mean that a component can really take a dousing. The system you choose might be a combination of, say, a marine-quality player with waterproof speakers for use on deck, and weather "resistant" speakers to install down below.

One company that specializes in marine stereo is Maxxima,

which uses weatherproof gaskets, silicone-sprayed components, a vibration-absorption system, and a protectively painted chassis. Maxxima's weatherproof speakers are made of polypropylene.

Jensen Marine Audio makes weatherproof speakers for use on deck; weather-resistant speakers to install in protected areas of the boat. Poly-Planar has a new polystyrene speaker which is rugged, corrosionproof, waterproof, and acoustically superior.

No longer do you have to settle for an automotive stereo, or a household system that you hope will hold up in the marine environment. Companies such as Maxxima offer all the bells and whistles including five-band equalizer, ten-station memory, double cassette recorder, fader, high-speed dubbing, and remote control from anywhere on board, plus such handy features as battery backup and marine weather bands.

In addition to choosing marine electronics where possible, and installing them correctly, it's important to protect tapes, CDs, and records from the elements and from dampness and temperature extremes when the boat is not in use. Keep them in a high, dry compartment; off-season, take them home. With so many attractive, convenient tape carriers on the market, some families find it better to take tapes home when they leave the boat and bring fresh, new programs with them when they come back aboard.

If you're looking for a theftproof unit for use in an unlockable part of the boat, Pioneer Sound makes a tough radio/tape player designed for sport vehicles. Its quick release feature allows the head unit to be removed, so you can lock it down below when leaving the boat. Called Truck Rider, it's available from 12 Volt Catalog, 110 E. Atlantic Ave., Delray Beach, FL 33444.

Adventures in Space

Entire books can be written on the placement and installation of entertainment electronics. It's an assignment that should be worked out with your decorator and/or your electrician early in any boat-building or redecorating project. Wiring has to be planned for; speakers may have to be built into overheads, cabinets, bulkheads, or furniture.

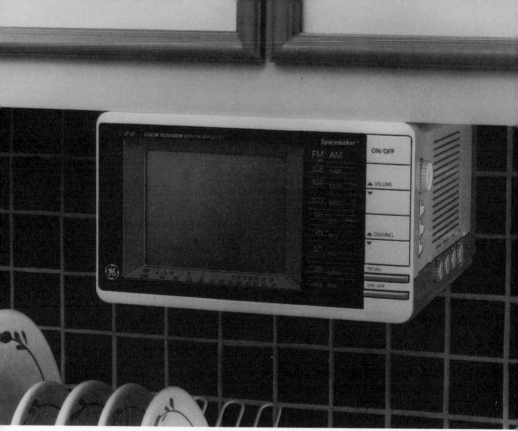

Spacemaker appliances are compact and top-mounted. They ride securely, and are ideal for use in available nooks and crannies. GENERAL ELECTRIC

A helpful booklet on selecting equipment is available from the Electronic Industries Assn., 1722 Eye St., Suite 200, Washington, DC 20006. Enclose a stamped, self-addressed, business-size envelope, and a note asking for a booklet on whatever equipment interests you.

Begin your planning by listing everything you want your entertainment center to contain. It may be a very long list including projection TV, video games, music systems, speakers on deck and in every cabin, and more. Then, decide whether some or all of it will be run on 110 volts. Finally, determine how it can be fit in physically, esthetically, and for best audio quality.

You'll need safe, secure mounting for each piece of equipment, appropriate wiring behind the scenes, and protected shelves or storage lockers for tapes, records, remotes, and other accessories. Swivel TV mounts, which allow viewing from different angles, are available through marine stores and camping suppliers.

Controls should be easily accessible, so front-mounted controls will be best for units that will be mounted and installed in tight spots. Controls for remote-control components can be less convenient. Cabinetry should be designed to secure and to protect equipment, and perhaps to screen it from sight when not in use (if you don't like the cold eye of an unused TV staring at you), but it should also allow plenty of ventilation so heat doesn't build up in the equipment.

What's Available

Camping World, P.O. Box 90017, Bowling Green, KY 42102 (write for free catalog) offers a thirteen-inch color TV with built-in VCR, and an AC/DC video player. If you will be using all 110V equipment, Camping World offers a pocket-size inverter that puts out 100 watts continuous, 200 watts peak. Larger and more sophisticated inverters (to convert ships battery power to 110 volts) are available through marine suppliers.

AC/DC television and videocassette players are also available from 12 Volt Products Inc., Box 664, Holland, PA 18966, and the 12 Volt Catalog, address above.

Philips Consumer Electronics, P.O. Box 14810, Knoxville, TN 37914 offers, in addition to many other electronics, the Magnavox Picture-in-Picture Observation System that allows surveillance of a selected area (such as the deck, or a child's cabin) while watching TV.

General Electric's Spacemaker television/radio, designed for under-counter installation, is a good choice for the galley or for individual cabins. It's held securely by a mount that allows it to turn for best viewing, and easily removes from the mount for viewing elsewhere. Useful contacts:

Jensen Marine Audio, (800)323-0707.

Niles Audio Corporation, (305)238-4373. Bulkhead-mounted speakers.

Poly-Planar Inc. 1800 Mearns Rd., Warminster, PA 18974.

Si-Tex Marine Stereo, P.O. Box 6700, Clearwater, FL 34618.

Sharp Electronics, Sharp Plaza, Mahwah, NJ 07430.

Carrier, United Technologies, (800)227-7437. Makes electronic air purifiers.

Sony Corporation, Corporate Communications, 9 W. 57th St., New York, NY 10019. Inquire about the Sony Mariner line.

Alarm Systems

Advances in security systems have been as fast-paced as those in other electronics. Some are mere gimmicks; others are so complex that you can't figure them out, or they cry *Wolf!* so often that nobody pays attention, or they're constantly on the fritz. To find an effective, foolproof alarm system is not easy. If possible, have

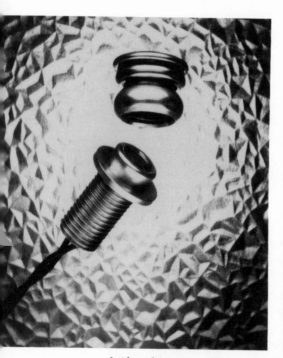

A tiny brass switch installs in a boat snap, and sounds an alarm if anyone unsnaps a boat cover to enter your boat. It sounds an audible alarm, prevents engine start, and is capable of police department tie-in. BOAT SENTRY

your electrician design a system specifically for your boat, its furnishings, and your life-style.

If you're buying a ready-made alarm system, get one designed for marine use. You need an alarm that won't drain batteries when you're not aboard, that won't be triggered by the boat's natural movements, and that won't pack up at the first sniff of salt air. The alarm must also suit special purposes, which could mean anything from blowing a siren to preventing engine start.

Marine burglar alarms are offered by Boat/US and other catalogs. If your marine electrician is designing a system just for you, consider such extras as fire sensors, high-water alarms, a high-temperature alarm in the refrigerator or freezer, intrusion alarms, and individual protection for special items such as expensive electronics, the dingy, and the outboard.

Among offbeat systems are:

Boat Sentry, 271 Rt. 46 West, Fairfield, NJ 07006, makers of marine alarm systems, makes a switch sensor which is magnetically seated and fits into a cockpit snap cover. After detecting intrusion, it sounds and alarm and blocks engine ignition.

Hammacher Schlemmer stores sell an easy-to-use alarm designed for sliding doors like those found in many houseboats and cruisers.

Rabbit Systems, 100 Wilshire Blvd., Santa Monica, CA 90401. Automotive security systems including one that looks like a teddy bear.

Shop home-improvement stores for the newest smoke detectors. Many types and styles are now available.

Chapter 13

ABOUT LOCKERS

Cupboards, drawers, clothes closets, the linen closet, a tool bin, a medicine cabinet.

In household parlance we use a great many terms for places where things are kept. Aboard your boat, they're all called simply lockers but your storage needs on board are far more complex and demanding than they are at home. Things must be kept dry, handy, protected from shifting underway, and well aired. And, because stowage space is always too small, no matter how big the boat, you have to make maximum use of every bin and bilge, locker and lazarette, cupboard and cubbyhole.

Hanging Lockers

• Keep foul-weather gear in a separate locker, as far from everything else as possible. Once wet with salt water, storm wear never dries completely because salt residue continues to draw moisture out of the air. Ideally, the oilskin locker is handy to the companionway and has its own drain into the bilge. If possible, provide a way to stow foul-weather boots upside down where they can drain and dry.

166

Shop closet-accessory departments in stores and home-improvement centers for the best variety in space extenders.

One way to increase access to a deep, narrow hanging locker is through the use of a carousel. This 110V unit fits closets that are at least 4'6" × 7'. Construction is aluminum, plastic, and nylon.

WHITE HOME PRODUCTS

167

- Breathable canvas clothing bags will protect dressy garments from the everyday jostle.
- Avoid plastic garment bags, shoe bags, and other closet organizers. They seal in moisture so shoes mildew faster and clothes get musty. The bags get brittle and break down within a year or two. Nylon fabric clothing bags and organizers cost more, last longer, and breathe.
- Check the Sears catalog for closet organizers. Systems include a pocketed nylon bag and a hang-up system that consists of a series of stretchable mesh compartments. Sears also sells a variety of organizer systems which hang over doors. Specialty catalogs such as *Hold Everything* (see Chapter 14) are also good sources of stowage aids.
- Investigate the many new styles in closet hardware. Even after eliminating the many types of cheap cardboard and uncoated steel accessories, you'll find many household closet space-expanders that will make lockers more efficient. Home-improvement stores and closet-accessories departments in large department stores are good sources of the more durable types.
- Moths go to sea, too. If possible, line one or two clothes lockers with cedar boards. Ready-made cedar closet liner sets are available in home-improvement stores. Cut leftover cedar boards into sections eight inches or ten inches long and place one in each compartment of a shoe bag.
- Ventilate, ventilate, ventilate the shelves, the locker door, bulkheads, and the shoe racks. Coated wire or plank shelving is strong, and allows far more air flow than solid wood or composite shelves.
- Two of the most imaginative boat redecorators I've ever met are Annie and Bob Bolderson. Aboard their *Nymph Errant,* the master stateroom had a deep, narrow closet that would have accommodated a rod only about sixteen inches wide—enough to hold only a dozen garments or so. So, they devised a sliding rod that filled the entire depth of the closet, creating a rack that was three times longer than they could have had with a conventional closet rod. To find or replace a garment, they simply

Coated-wire closet systems can be used to customize and ventilate hanging lockers and make the best use of available space. CLOSET MAID

Coated-steel closet accessories can often be adapted for boat use. Plank-style shelving is stronger; wire-style shelving allows more air exchange. To prevent rust, touch up any spots where steel is exposed. Use a suitable paint or coating.
STANLEY HARDWARE

pulled the entire rod, drawer-like, into the cabin. Hardware for such pull-out installations is found in home-improvement stores and in specialty woodworking catalogs.

• Long-distance sailors know that it's not uncommon for a garment to develop holes from the constant swinging and abrasion during a long passage. Use good hangers—the padded satin type, heavy plastic, or smoothly varnished (not unfinished) wood. Use straps or bungee cord to secure rows of hanging clothes underway.

• Often a closet can be made more usable, if not roomier, by changing or removing a door. I find sliding doors a poor choice for boat closets because you can never open more than half the closet at one time. If these doors are also mirrored, a popular designer choice, they have the added debit of having no vent holes.

The advantage of a strong, conventional, hinged door is that it opens completely. On both sides, or perhaps just on the back side, you can install all sorts of organizers from belt and tie racks to shoe bags or a full-length mirror. Folding or sliding doors don't offer these extra storage areas. If you are adding a lot of heavy storage to such doors (e.g., storage shelving or baskets) use heavy-duty hinges.

Another option is to remove the doors on a small hanging locker. While it's hard to improve on the looks of a neatly enclosed closet, you'll have more ventilation, and easier access to your clothes, if the doors are discarded.

Consider replacing them with, say, a round or oval frame that gives the opening a finished look. Aboard our boat *Sans Souci,* the hanging locker had such a frame. Straps were snapped across it to keep clothes from swinging underway. Another option for a small closet door is a roll-away closure like that on a rolltop desk. Tambour laminates are available in both colors and woods. The door could roll to the top, bottom, or either side, completely out of the way.

• Wireless, inexpensive battery-operated closet lights are available from specialty catalogs and from discount stores. They simply screw to any available bulkhead or overhead. Or, get a clip-on, battery-operated reading light and attach it somewhere in the closet. Another choice is to install a deck prism that will light the closet, at least during the day. The more light you can provide in a crowded closet, the easier it will be to find things.

Drawer Storage

• Add ventilating holes to drawers and drawer fronts as much as is practical. As a decorative device, drawer fronts could be made of basketweave teak or wicker. Or, use insert panels made of chair caning material.

• Many new boats have molded plastic drawers with wood fronts. They look good, clean easily, and have no rough edges to snag sweaters or lingerie. If you're adding drawers anywhere in your boat, shop around to see if a molded plastic box or drawer is available to fit.

• Odd-lot rolls of wallpaper are a pretty, inexpensive choice for drawer lining. Wallpaper is thick and absorbent so it is a better choice than plastic shelf liner material.

• Foam drawer-liner material, intended for use in tool boxes, is sold in hardware stores and tool departments. It makes a sound-dampening, nonskid liner for drawers and cupboards everywhere in the boat. Disposable, puffy paper material, sold in some marine stores as nonskid placemats, also makes good drawer liners. It is the same material used as placemats on many airliners.

• Wherever possible, install drawers, which are cheaper and easier, instead of a cupboard or bin. The advantage to a drawer versus a cupboard is that it can be removed completely for sorting, searching, and cleaning. I'm amazed at how much easier it is to retrieve pots and pans now that I keep them in the big drawers suggested by my designer. Instead of reaching back, back into the depths of a cavernous locker to wrestle out a big pressure cooker or lobster pot, I just pull out the drawer and there are all my pans.

Extra-heavy drawer rollers are available through specialty woodworking catalogs, so don't think that drawers are only for lightweight items. They can also be used for heavy pots, tools, or heavy electronic items.

Linen Closet

- I stopped using formaldehyde mildew preventives because of their sharp, lingering smell. It took several launderings to remove it from some linens I'd stored. I've never had much faith either in those hygroscopic materials which draw moisture from the air and collect it in a plastic tub (the tub and the moisture remain in your closet).

  Alternatives: Empty drawers every few months and wash them with a mildewcide bathroom cleaner. Dry well, then refill with clean clothes.

  Install low-wattage heating rods (see Chapter 14) in storage areas. Where practical, run air conditioning or a dehumidifier on the boat when you're not aboard and, where possible, install extra ventilators over locker areas.
- Continually rotate stored linens, putting the freshly laundered items on the bottom and bringing those that were stored longest to the top.
- Never put anything away unless it is bone-dry.
- Plastic-coated steel wire shelving sold in home stores lets linens breathe. In the home, it's installed lip down because the lip doubles as a hanger bar. Install it upside down on the boat, with the lip up, and you'll have a two-inch rail to keep items from sliding off.

Other Tips About Lockers

- The more you can isolate the chain locker from the living areas of the boat, the better. Each time you stow the anchor rode, you're bringing gallons of wetness into the boat. The chain locker needs plenty of ventilation and drainage; the boat will stay dryer if you can vent it to the outdoors.
- While it's always tempting and often more practical to divide all stowage areas into neat shelves and pigeon-holes, it's sometimes better to leave big storage areas, such as those under bunks or dinette seas, undivided. Stowage modules, in whatever sizes are needed for the purpose, can be added and shuffled around as needed.

  Suitable modules include plastic wastebaskets for deep areas that have top access; dishpans to hold hand

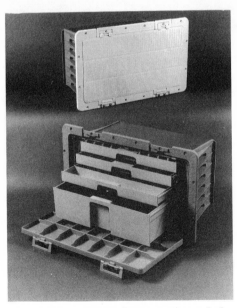

Tempress now makes a line of storage modules that are easy to build into the boat. A fairly crude cut-out will do because the modules have their own, handsome flanges.
TEMPRESS INC.

173

towels and dry foods; plastic "milk carriers" to hold canned goods; and, for stacking, lidded plastic sweater or blanket boxes or Rubbermaid's Roughneck line of heavy-duty containers with sturdy lids.

- If elegance is important to you, have it! One of my sailing friends has a set of Baccarat crystal aboard; aboard a fabulous Feadship, I saw that an entire set of Waterford crystal glasses was carried in custom cupboards with leaded glass doors. Each piece of fragile china and crystal must, of course, have its own slot. It takes a lot of space, but any competent ship's carpenter can design such stowage for you.

- Make suitable cutouts in a cupboard or drawer for liquor storage. Or, for round bottles, use lengths of plastic pipe in suitable diameters, as drawer dividers. Don't forget to design horizontal wine-bottle storage into a cool spot where it will get the least movement. Light, heat, and motion are all enemies of fine wines.

- Plastic tackle boxes make practical and portable storage boxes for sewing supplies, small parts and spares, and first-aid supplies.

- Don't stow items that can be utilized if left out in the open. Down jackets, comforters, extra pillows, and sleeping bags can be stuffed into pillow shams and used as throw pillows. Stacks of floating cushions can be placed in a canvas "box" and used as hassocks. The big salad bowl that you use only when you have guests aboard can be used daily as a centerpiece fruit bowl or catch-all.

- Fiddles (protective rails) are a must on all but the most tame waterways, to keep dishes from falling off the counter and table, to keep books from falling out of book cases, and to keep pots on the stove. Where possible, design fiddles that are removable. Cleaning will be easier, and the fiddles can be put away when you're dockside and don't need them.

Chapter 14

USEFUL ADDRESSES

Dressing Ship

A yacht is "dressed" with the proper flags. A full line of ensigns, signals, and novelty flags is offered by Dettra Flag Company Inc., Oaks, PA 19456.

Galley Equipment

Avery Services, 905 E. Second St., Los Angeles, CA 90012, (213)624-7832. Sells restaurant equipment, mostly to the trade but is open to the public. More than three hundred kinds of equipment featured, from pretzel warmers to hot-chocolate dispensers. Name brands in appliances, cookware, imports.

Chiswick, 33 Union Ave., Sudbury, MA 01776. Industrial supplier of containers, wrapping materials, extra-heavy-duty plastic zip-top bags in all sizes, perforated rubber antifatigue matting.

Key Line Sales Inc., P.O. Box 1861, Elkhart, IN 46515. Manufacturers representative offering single and double stainless-steel sinks in various configurations.

Marine Appliances International, 2807 Antigue Dr., Burbank, CA 91505. Marine appliances including hard-to-find 12V automatic icemaker.

S. E. Rykoff and Company, P.O. Box 21467, Los Angeles, CA 90021. Free catalog, mostly devoted to fancy foods but some hard-to-find galley items such as restaurant-quality Silverstone saute pans and commercial-grade stainless-steel cookpots.

Sailing Angles, Inc., P.O. Box 331725, Coconut Grove, FL 33133. Nonskid products including foam drawer liner, dish disks, self-adhesive liners.

SeaWard, P.O. Box 566, La Puente, CA 91747. Full line of galley stoves including Hillerange, Princess, Litton; also marine water heaters and propane accessories.

Spiegel, 1040 W. 35th St., Chicago, IL 60672. Catalog $5. Very good collection of upscale, unusual galleyware and microware including microwave waffler and sandwich maker.

Fabrics

John Boyle and Company Inc., P.O. Box 791, Statesville, NC 28677, (704)872-8151. Marine fabrics and fasteners.

Reliatex, 6004 Bonacker Dr., Tampa, FL 33610, (813)621-6021 or (800)282-9121. Distributors and fabricators of marine fabrics, foams, findings. Write or call for information on where to buy marine fabrics in your area.

Furniture

Glen Eagle Furniture, Statesville, NC 28677, (704)873-3244.

Hutton Furniture Company, P.O. Box 158, Hickory, NC 28603, (704)322-3330.

Santa Barbara Designs, P.O. Box 90610, Santa Barbara, CA 93190. Prestige line of patio furniture in teak.

Southern Moldings, Industrial Park Rd., Frankfurt KY, (502)695-2800, distributes Quick Bed, an Australian sofabed that flicks open with a touch. Unlike conventional sofabeds, this one has no outer frame to bark shins.

Hardware

Glide-Tape Drapery System. Create crisp, pleated draperies that install on a rustproof track. Shapco, 4304 Regency Dr., Glenview, IL 60025.

Grohe America Inc., 900 Lively Blvd., Wood Dale, IL 60191. Extensive selection of multipurpose marine faucets with pullout shower spray.

Kemp George, 306 Dartmouth St., Boston, MA 02116, (800)343-4012. Custom treatments for head and galley include solid brass, polished brass bar sink, premium-quality porcelains and chromes, hard-to-find antique reproductions. Catalog.

Renovator's Supply, Millers Falls, MA 01349, (413)659-2211. Catalog of hardware, plumbing, and light fixtures in period and hard-to-find sizes and styles, many available in solid brass.

Lighting

Hella, Inc. P.O. Box 1064, Cranford, NJ 07016. Manufacturers of marine interior and exterior lighting, horns, warning horns, and accessories.

Thin-Lite Corporation, 530 Constitution Ave., Camarillo, CA 93010. Extensive line of space-efficient 12V interior lights, bulbs, fixtures.

Miscellaneous Accessories

American Foreign Industries, 1085 Shary Circle, Concord, CA 94518. Teak furniture and accessories.

Basic Designs Inc., 5815 Bennett Valley Rd., Santa Rosa, CA 95404. Request price list for unusual accessories including Sun Shower, mattress, pillow.

Boat/US, 880 Pickett St., Alexandria, VA 22304. Membership organization offers complete catalog of marine gear at discount prices. Also lobbies for boatmen's rights, offers discount insurances, provides towing service, etc.

Camping World, P.O. Box 90017, Bowling Green, KY, 42102, (800)626-5944 in U.S. and Canada. Catalog. Retail stores in South, West, Michigan, Kentucky. Large selection of 12V appliances, butane-fired iron, folding bicycles, compact combination washer-dryer, and other RV equipment which can be used in yachts.

Coast Navigation, 116 Legion Ave., Annapolis, MD 21401. Clothing, electronics, gadgets, teak accessories, brass lamps, interior light fixtures.

W. H. Den Ouden (U.S.A.) Inc., P.O. Box 8712, Baltimore, MD 21240. Includes Vetus, Budget Marine. Wide variety of high-quality, Dutch-made accessories, furnishings.

Elkhart Door Inc., P.O. Box 2177, Elkhart, IN 46515. Window treatments, light fixtures, and wood or imitation wood folding doors.

Golden Rod, Buenger Enterprises, P.O. Box 5286, Oxnard, CA 93031. Plug-in heater rods 12"–36" drawing 8–25 watts, delivering continuous, mild heat to banish dampness in enclosed areas. Smallest model covers up to 100 cubic feet; largest up to 500 cubic feet.

Hammacher Schlemmer, 212 S. Superior, Chicago, IL 60610. Send for a free catalog listing many unusual items including water-resistant cordless phone, rechargeable five-inch color television, hand-held vacuum cleaner, and a sliding door barrier alarm.

Herrington, 3 Symmes Dr., Londonderry, NH 03053. Unusual, up-market accessories for boats, cars, and golf. Include Nautical Sleep System custom sheets, portable air conditioner that fits over a hatch, desktop stereo, deck chairs. Send for free catalog.

Highsmith Company, P.O. Box 800, Fort Atkinson, WI 53538, (800)558-2110. Primarily office and library supplies but has very large choice of storage equipment to help organize lockers.

Hold Everything, P.O. Box 7807, San Francisco, CA 94120. Clever collections of storage aids and space stretchers that nest, stack, fold, disappear, protect, hold, or organize.

M&E Marine Supply Co., P.O. Box 601, Camden, NJ 08101, (800)541-6501. Discount marine supplies including long list of teak accessories, small galley stoves, acrylic glasses. Catalog. Showrooms in Glasgow, DE and Collingswood, NJ.

Outer Banks, P.O. Drawer 500, Beaufort, NC 28516, (800)682-2225. Free catalog of marine needs including deck furniture, teak accessories, clocks and barometers, brass lights.

12 Volt Catalog, 110 E. Atlantic Ave., Delray Beach, FL 33444. Good selection of 12V and solar equipment and stylish 12V light fixtures.

12 Volt Products Inc., P.O. Box 664, Holland PA 18966. Appliances, fans, lights, accessories. Send $2 for catalogue.

West Marine Products, P.O. Box 1020, Watsonville, CA 95077. Discount accessories. Free catalogue.

The Woodworkers' Store, 21801 Industrial Blvd., Rogers, MN 55374. Catalogue $1. Large selection of unusual hardware items and other woodworking aids that can aid in custom creation of the galley, closets, cabinets, furniture.

Professional associations that may be useful to you in locating products, information, sources, or lists of individual manufacturers include:

American Plywood Assn.
1119 A St.
Tacoma, WA 98401

American Textile Mfr. Assn.
400 S. Tryon
Charlotte, NC 28285

Canvas Products Assn.
600 Endicott Bldg.
St. Paul, MN 55101

Carpet and Rug Institute
P.O. Box 2048
Dalton, GA 30720

National Assn. Furniture Mfrs.
8401 Connecticut Ave.
Washington, DC 20015

National Decorating Products Assn.
9334 Dielman Ind. Dr.
St. Louis, MO 63132

National Hardwood Lumber Assn.
332 S. Michigan Ave.
Chicago, IL 60604

National Home Furnishing Assn.
405 Merchandise Mart
Chicago, IL 60654

National Housewares Mfr. Assn.
1130 Merchandise Mart
Chicago, IL 60654

Publications

Boating Digest, P.O. Box 661, Yarmouth, ME 04096. Free subscription to boat owners. Newspaper covering boating products.

Barris Marine, 135 Dolphin Dr., Woodmere, NY 11598. Boating books. Call (800)866-2326 and ask for book by title or for free catalog.

Marine Textiles, P.O. Box 720, Wayzata, MN 55391. Closed-circulation trade publication which you cannot get unless you're involved in the marine business. Excellent source of decorating, fabric, and carpeting information for yourself or your decorator.

Nynex Directories, 201 Edgewater Dr., Wakefield, MA 01880. Regional yellow pages–type directories listing supplier names and addresses by category, plus helpful charts and other boating information. Send for information on how to order current editions.

Software

Galley Slave, Doug Rose Associates, 8885 N. Atlantic Ave., Cape Canaveral FL 32920. A complete guide to provisioning and galley recipes. Send $49.95 for the program, postpaid.

While every effort has been made to provide current addresses and telephone numbers, they are highly perishable in today's mobile marine world. The reader in search of particular companies and products should allow time to contact several manufacturers, and perhaps to track down companies by telephone. (800) numbers given are not necessarily accessible from all calling areas.

INDEX

About the Author

Janet Groene lived with her husband, Gordon, aboard their own thirty-foot sloop for ten years while cruising Florida waters and the Bahamas. Avid do-it-yourselfers, they've always done most of their own work, from major refits to routine cleaning, updates, and reupholstering. Now a full-time writer and photographer team based in Florida, they write about travel, boating and yachting, and how-to for the home, shop, and boat.

Since moving back ashore, the Groenes (say GRAYnees) have built two homes and remodeled two others while writing for such magazines as *Homeowner* and *Remodeling*. Meanwhile, their travel-writing assignments take them all over the world on a wide variety of vessels.

They've cruised aboard expedition ships in Indonesia and the Arctic, taken crewed barges through England and Holland, and have bareboated under power and sail in England, Scotland, Australia, New Zealand, and the Caribbean. They have also houseboated widely in inland America and have cruised aboard larger ships in Mexico, Panama, Colombia, the Caribbean, the Bahamas, and Alaska.

Janet's acquaintance with boats spans from luxurious private, corporate, and commercial yachts to the most spartan and shopworn bareboats, to cruise liners. She brings to her writing a practical, hands-on knowledge of both boating and of decorating methods and materials.